Community under Stress

An Internment Camp Culture

COMMUNITY
UNDER
STRESS

An Internment Camp
Culture

BY ELIZABETH HEAD VAUGHAN

PRINCETON, NEW JERSEY
PRINCETON UNIVERSITY PRESS
1949

LONDON: GEOFFREY CUMBERLEGE, OXFORD UNIVERSITY PRESS

TO

Beth & Clay

THIS sociological study of a Japanese concentration camp in the Philippine Islands may be regarded as the report of an involuntary participant observer. It is a study of a social experiment unplanned by the author. The account is based upon a personal record kept day by day in the camp.

The author, a former research assistant in the Institute for Research in Social Science at the University of North Carolina, went to the Philippines to live in 1937. After teaching a year in the University of the Philippines, she married an American engineer and resided in the Visayan or middle group of the Islands. At the outbreak of war in the Far East in December, 1941, her husband enlisted in the United States Army, was captured by the Japanese on Bataan, and died shortly after in the Cabanatuan Military Prison.

The author and her two children, then aged one and two years, after several months of hiding with Negritos in the mountains of Negros Island, surrendered to the Japanese on June 7, 1942. They were interned with 145 other "enemy aliens" in an elementary school building in the major seaport town of the Island, Bacolod City. Included in the heterogeneous group brought together by the Japanese in Bacolod were white Americans, an American Negro, three American Indians (trapped en route from a California reservation to China), British, Dutch, and Filipinos. They were men, women, and children.

For nine months the Japanese failed to provide the Bacolod internees with food, and the group survived by pooling individually owned supplies and its labor resources.

On March 2, 1943, the Bacolod camp was discontinued

and the internees put aboard ship for Manila. They arrived at Santo Tomas camp on Luzon Island on March 10. The author and her two children remained in Santo Tomas with approximately four thousand other civilians of thirteen[1] nationalities until they were released by American forces on February 3, 1945. In April, 1945, the writer and her children were repatriated to the United States.

The walled-in internment camp became a laboratory in which mobility and association were rigidly controlled, and in which general conduct could be microscopically analyzed. Effects of the thwarting of both basic and acquired (cultural) drives upon personality and upon group organization evidenced themselves during the forced intimacies of imprisonment. As a result of the racial and cultural heterogeneity of the internee population, there developed within the confines of the camp an original cultural mosaic tessellated of both new and of previously established culture traits. Orientals and occidentals, primitive and civilized individuals, contributed to the development of new action patterns and new artifacts in an effort to meet the psychic and physical needs of the men, women, and children thrown together. The cultural configuration within the Bacolod camp was shaped largely through the direction of three groups of internees: (1) those closest to the Island way of life; (2) those with resourcefulness in developing manual and domestic skills; (3) those with theoretical knowledge of or actual experience in a non-monetary economy.

---

[1] In order of frequency: American (whites, Negroes, Indians); British (English, Scots, Australians, Indians, Canadians); Dutch (Hollanders, Malayans); Polish; Norwegian; Italian; French; Spanish; Egyptian; Swiss; German; Slovak; Nicaraguan.

Perhaps the most striking single conclusion drawn from the material presented in *Community under Stress* relates to the comparative effects of internment upon women and men. According to certain objectively determinable gauges, i.e., participation in or withdrawal from the internee-initiated camp program, actual and percentage losses in weight, mental breakdowns, deaths from disease, and suicides, women seemed to adjust more readily to the internment situation than did men. Camp living conditions were almost identical for the sexes, with food rationing balanced in favor of the men who performed the heaviest physical tasks. Age differences of the sexes were not significant.

During the three years of internment adult weight losses totaled 70,000 pounds, or 35 tons, with a greater actual and greater percentage weight loss among men than women. During this same period, of deaths by disease (exclusive of deaths from enemy torture or shelling) in a population 61 per cent male, 89.5 per cent of the deaths were male. The female population (39 per cent of the total) suffered but 10.5 per cent of deaths from illness. All suicides were male. Man's prestige as "protector of women and children" suffered by internment, and business and financial worries preyed heavily upon the men. On the other hand, the traditional self-sacrifice and resignation expected of women aided in adjustment to the internee role.

Young children did not experience during internment the subjective feeling of frustration which was characteristic of adults. Among adolescents, however, the personal denials incurred during three years of internment were keenly sensed. Teen-age internees were aware of the maturing influences of internment, which would make it difficult for them, after release, to prolong with gratification the academic and social activities interrupted by the war. Yet, in general, biological factors of sex, age, or race, were less significant influences upon adjustment than were the cultural backgrounds of the individuals and groups studied.

The development of a communal system of government within the Bacolod camp is a story in itself. The leadership which emerged spontaneously was interracial and cross-sectional, contingent upon a willingness to serve the group without remuneration. The development of artifacts—essential and ornamentative—gave evidence that the camp environment actually fostered the expression of certain practical and ingenious capabilities held latent by modern technological civilization.

Certain acknowledgments are due to those whose interest and assistance have made this book possible. First, I wish to acknowledge my great indebtedness to Dr. Howard W. Odum, head of the Department of Sociology and Anthropology at the University of North Carolina. He was a constant source of encouragement and stimulation during the preparation of this manuscript. Dr. Gordon W. Blackwell, Director, and Dr. John Gillin and Dr. Katharine Jocher, of the Institute for Research in Social Science at the University of North Carolina, were a committee of three who read and constructively criticized the original manuscript which was submitted as a dissertation requirement for the doctorate degree from the Department of Sociology and Anthropology of the University of North Carolina. Their suggestions have been invaluable.

Dr. Erwin H. Ackerknecht of the University of Wisconsin prepared for my use a report on his own internment experience in a civilian camp in France. Material from this report has been incorporated within the manuscript. Mr. George M. Bridgeford of Manila, P.I., added to the information concerning the pre-war Island culture. The Julius Rosenwald Foundation was the donor of a grant which made possible the preparation of this book.

Contents

Tables and Illustrations

Community under Stress

An Internment Camp Culture

1

Introduction

"OBJECTIVITY" and "subjectivity" are in failing repute as wholly commendatory or wholly condemnatory attributes of social research. To say that complete objectivity is possible in such a study as this would, I believe, be false representation, yet objectivity has been attempted. During the enforced participation within a social situation which made uncertain the continuance of life itself, complete detachment from that situation was impossible. As the participant observer technique employed voluntarily in studies of primitive cultures and of contemporary societies has yielded impersonal, unbiased interpretation and evaluation of the human behavior under consideration, so, it seems to me, the same technique may be applied even more advantageously in an involuntary situation such as internment.

One need not accept the objectivity hypotheses of Lundberg to ask with him, "At what point exactly . . . does the mysterious transition from outside to inside of one's material take place?"[1] It is a tenet of psychology and sociology that a sensation or an emotion need not be experienced by the observer for its results in others to be recorded in accurately descriptive terminology. In this study, however, I discovered that an acutely realistic understanding of the effects of hunger upon personality was made possible by a personal sensation of hunger.

Research fields are seldom limited to male or to female investigators. Yet, social situations of such nature arise that

[1] George A. Lundberg, "Can Science Save Us?" *Harper's Magazine,* CXCI (1945), 527.

sometimes members of one sex or the other have more ready access to information relating to the situation. The bulk of the reports of war imprisonment have been the records of men—about themselves and other men.[2] Published analyses of prisoner-of-war situations have been concerned primarily with military rather than civilian populations. General materials relating to the war imprisonment experience have come more often from the British than from the American press,[3] and scientific reports have approached the subject more frequently from the medical (psychiatric) viewpoint than from that of sociology. However, the study of the adaptations of individuals and groups to a new cultural situation is clearly within the scope of the latter.

The contemporary approach in studies of war imprisonment is still primarily psychiatric. It is, in the main, an individual, diagnostic approach with therapeutic ends rather than a seeking of an interpretation of the social and cultural processes functioning within an interned group.

The purpose of this study is to throw light upon the following questions: How has modern civilization equipped or handicapped men and women for survival within an internment camp environment?[4] What are the ideologies regarding the equalization of property which seem to diffuse

---

[2] The Library of Congress (Division of Bibliography) has issued a list of miscellaneous publications dealing with prison camp experiences during World War I. With one exception these publications relate to camps for males only. See Appendix.

[3] *Ibid.* Of the publications listed in the Library of Congress, 68 per cent are of British, 18 per cent of French, and 14 per cent of American origin.

[4] Whereas the term "imprisonment" may refer to military or civilian populations, the term "prison camp" is generally used with reference to military prisons only. "Internment camp" and "concentration camp" apply to centers of civilian incarceration.

within a group suffering disaster? What is the basis of leadership in a crisis situation when former status and role diminish in significance? What are the acculturation processes of a group making substitutions for or replacing the necessities of daily living which are suddenly denied it? When solitude and privacy (as fundamental human demands as the need for companionship) are lacking, what is the effect upon the individual and the group? Who finds adjustment to life behind barbed wire most difficult: men, women, or children?

The modern civilian internment camp for the large scale retention of noncombatants might rightly be called an excrescence of military strategy. The military-civilian dichotomy which was maintained throughout World War II did not prevent unwanted resident civilian populations from being compelled by military policy and exigency into conditions of mass confinement. This was true in Belsen in Europe, Santo Tomas in the Philippines, and Fort Missoula in the United States—to mention but a few scattered concentration centers.

The earliest International Convention that relates specifically to the treatment of prisoners of war is to be found in the Annex to the Hague Convention II of 1899, setting forth the Laws and Customs of War on Land. This convention was ratified or adhered to without reservation by 46 of the leading nations of the world. The Hague Convention II of 1899 was followed, and in effect supplemented, by the Hague Convention IV of 1907, which covered the same subject matter.[5]

[5] *Liberated Military Personnel*, "Report of Claims Committee" (American Bldg., Washington, D.C., 1946), p. 3.

The Geneva Convention of July, 1929, recognized the rights of the military captor over enemy captives of war and concerned itself with amelioration of the lot of the prisoner. The convention specifies that "Prisoners of war are in the power of the hostile power, but not of the individuals or corps who have captured them,"[6] and details methods of prisoner treatment.

The Geneva Convention of 1929, signed by 47 nations (including the United States, Germany, and Japan) has but one reference to civilians—"individuals who follow armed forces without directly belonging thereto, such as newspaper correspondents and reporters, sutlers, contractors"[7]—and states that these shall be treated as military prisoners of war, leaving the application of the terms of the convention to general noncombatant internees as a matter of national option. Though both the United States and Japan were signatory powers, and the convention was ratified by the United States government in 1932, the Japanese failed to ratify the convention. Hence the United States was not bound to observe the terms of the convention in its treatment of Japanese prisoners during World War II.[8] "Concern over the treatment of American prisoners of war and civilians in Japanese hands, however, prompted a different policy. Early in the war the State Department obtained the Japanese Government's agreement to reciprocal application of the provisions of the Convention to prisoners of war, and insofar as the provisions of the Convention were

[6] "Treaty Conventions, International Acts, Protocols," *United States Senate Document 134*, IV (1923-37), 5229.

[7] *Ibid.*

[8] *United States Department of the Interior*, War Relocation Authority, "Legal and Constitutional Phases of the War Relocation Authority Program" (Washington, D.C., 1947), p. 18.

adaptable, to 'civilian internees.' "[9] It is interesting to note that, after this agreement, Japan and the United States each complained to the other of violations of the convention in the treatment of civilians.

During World War II wide variations in internment camp policy occurred between nations and between camps within a single nation. Both the manner and degree of outside administrative controls were important in determining the limits of variability for the different internment camp cultures. Camps were, in general, isolated from each other and from the rest of the world. In the Philippines each camp was an independent administrative entity unto itself. There was no over-all policy of camp administration as outlined by the Geneva Convention.[10]

During 1942 the Japanese maintained in the Philippine Islands civilian camps at Manila and Baguio on Luzon Island, Cebu on Cebu Island, Iloilo on Panay, Bacolod on Negros, and Davao on Mindanao. By the end of 1943 these camps, with the exception of Baguio, were closed and internees transferred to Santo Tomas camp in Manila. From Santo Tomas, groups of men, women, and children were later moved to Los Baños, also on Luzon Island, civilian males of military age being transferred first. All civilian internees in the Philippines were freed by the United States Army in February, 1945.

[9] *Ibid.*

[10] However, there was a tacit acknowledgment by the Japanese of an over-all policy. A General Kus was during 1944-45 in charge of all camps, military and civilian, succeeding General Movimoto. After the war's end General Kus was convicted and executed as a war criminal on the grounds that his was the implied responsibility for the treatment of the people in all camps.

The Santo Tomas camp culture was well established when the Bacolod men, women, and children were transferred to Manila in 1943. The culture nascency struggles observable in Bacolod were no longer evident in the smoothly functioning Santo Tomas camp system. Therefore the major part of this study is devoted to an analysis of developments within the smaller group on Negros Island.

2

Social and Economic Structure of the Philippines at Outbreak of War

OF THE sixteen million residents of the Philippine Islands at the outbreak of war approximately 15,800,000 were native born and of native stock. (See Table 1.) Chinese, Japanese, Americans were in that order next in Island population[1] but these and all other foreign groups made up less than three per cent of the total population.

The Philippines was a country of orientals.[2] White faces were few and generally concentrated in large cities. The exceptions to such white urbanization were the small, isolated special interest communities which dotted the Islands where a Caucasian-staffed sugar central, a lumber mill, or a missionary college had sprung up. Chief business interests of white skinned foreigners were export and import—the taking out of the Island agricultural and mineral products and the bringing in of religion and of American luxuries of living.

Both the national flag and seal of the Philippines bear three stars, evidence of major geographic and social divisions within the Islands: Luzon, the Visayas, and Mindanao. Luzon houses rice eating Tagalogs and Ilocanos, whose tribe names also designate the dialects they speak. Visayan people, with a distinct language and a corn as well as rice culture, occupy Negros, Cebu, Panay, and smaller

[1] "Commonwealth of the Philippines," *Statesman's Year Book*, LXXXI (1944), 672-678.
[2] Trinidad A. Rojo, "Philippine Population Problems," *Philippine Social Science Review*, XI (1939), 146.

TABLE I

Total, Foreign-born, and Mixed Population of the Philippines, by Provinces, 1939*

Province	Total	Foreign-born	Mixed
Philippines	16,000,303	165,813	50,519
Abra	87,780	95	41
Agusan	99,023	403	174
Albay	432,465	2,204	1,833
Antique	199,414	243	431
Bataan	85,538	90	86
Batanes	9,512	5	1
Batangas	442,034	949	234
Bohol	491,608	892	588
Bukidnon	57,561	158	96
Bulacan	332,807	611	360
Cagayan	292,270	1,603	864
Camarines Norte	98,324	2,065	541
Camarines Sur	385,695	2,350	1,156
Capiz	405,285	797	349
Cavite	238,581	1,735	763
Cebu	1,068,078	7,470	3,220
Cotabato	298,935	1,852	1,010
Davao	292,600	21,775	1,962
Ilocos Norte	237,586	449	185
Ilocos Sur	271,532	819	292
Iloilo	744,022	4,707	1,961
Isabela	219,864	1,961	940
La Union	207,701	618	351
Laguna	279,505	2,285	682
Lanao	243,437	674	530
Leyte	915,853	3,346	2,347
Manila, City of	623,492	58,766	7,517

Province	Total	Foreign-born	Mixed
Marinduque	81,768	574	115
Masbate	182,483	1,021	635
Mindoro	131,569	577	172
Misamis Occidental	210,057	1,112	838
Misamis Oriental	213,812	1,754	943
Mountain Province	296,874	3,532	1,005
Negros Occidental†	824,858	3,812	2,589
Negros Oriental	394,680	1,379	1,424
Nueva Ecija	416,762	1,468	466
Nueva Vizcaya	78,505	339	96
Palawan	93,673	574	286
Pampanga	375,281	1,583	703
Pangasinan	742,475	2,063	692
Rizal	444,805	9,063	3,007
Romblon	99,367	228	209
Samar	546,306	2,047	1,510
Sorsogon	247,653	1,544	1,422
Sulu	247,117	1,376	1,046
Surigao	225,895	1,358	716
Tarlac	264,379	1,528	488
Tayabas	358,553	4,295	838
Zambales	106,945	763	407
Zamboanga	355,984	4,901	2,398

* "The mixed (or mestizo) population is defined as persons whose fathers and mothers belong to different races. Persons whose father and/or mother were mestizos were to be reported as belonging to whichever race predominates. The persons reported as mixed (mestizos) include largely persons whose mother belongs to the brown race and whose father belongs to the yellow or white race. A large proportion of the persons reported as mixed are sons or daughters of a Filipino mother and a Chinese father. The categories 'foreign born' and 'mixed' are not necessarily mutually exclusive." "Summary Volume of the 1939 Census of the Philippines," Bureau of the Census, *United States Department of Commerce*, Washington, D.C. Quoted in letter from Leon E. Truesdell, Bureau of the Census (Washington, D.C.), July 8, 1946.

† Negros Island is divided into two provinces: Negros Occidental and Negros Oriental. Bacolod is located in Negros Occidental, which province contains approximately two-thirds of the Island population.

islands in the central Philippine area. To the far south, on Mindanao, Moros maintain after centuries of exposure to Christian influence a stronghold of Mohammedanism with customs and language unlike those found in other of the Islands.

The Chinese were among the first known foreign invaders of the Islands. They came as pirates and after successful piratical attacks settled along the Philippine coasts from Luzon to Mindanao. They intermarried with Filipinos and from restless seafaring turned to bartering and merchandising. While Filipinos fished, worked their rice paddies, and uninterruptedly worshiped their own gods, the Chinese entrenched themselves as the early trading class of the Islands.

The Spanish flag was planted in the Philippines in 1521, and with equal zeal the Spanish introduced a new religion and new agricultural methods. Filipino souls were directed toward a Christian heaven while their bodies were bent to slave labor. However, Spanish occupation did not stop Chinese attacks upon the Islands, and the Chinese sacked Manila while it was in Spanish hands. The persistence of the Chinese was matched only by the ruthlessness of the Spanish in the pillaging of Island wealth. The entrance of America into Philippine history brought about the withdrawal of organized Spanish troops but the unorganized Chinese were there to stay. Their proximity to the Islands allowed continual slipping in under cover of darkness.

The Spanish-American treaty of 1899 directed Filipino interests toward pure drinking water and education. Health and schools were introduced along with Protestantism, automobiles, and self-government.

American prestige in the Philippines flowered as the result of a liberal colonial policy and a well-presented display of materialistic treasures. Within the Islands the desirability of goods American eased the acceptance of ideas American. Typhoid injections and the substitution of the outdoor toilet for the pig under the hole in the kitchen floor were tolerated because the idiosyncratic Americans who demanded these brought materials with them to stimulate the Filipino's vanity and add comfort to his life. But the too-rapid advancement of American commerce and industry in the Islands, along with the increasing recognition by the Filipinos of the value of their own resources, soon tarnished the American prestige of the early quarter of the century. Americans came to be less appreciated as the liberators from Spanish tyrants as time and progress forced the period of tyranny into obscurity. The position of the Chinese in the Philippine economy likewise came under the scrutiny of the Islanders. Self-assertiveness taught by Americans resulted in the Filipino's taking stock of himself and his own opportunities in his homeland.

Negros Island, where the Bacolod camp was situated, is in the middle, or Visayan group, of the Philippines. Negros had felt the influence of both Chinese and Spanish invasions before American capital turned it into the sugar bowl of the Islands. At the outbreak of World War II descendants of the original Chinese merchants stood behind tienda counters at every road intersection, and lines of chanting followers of Our Lady of Lourdes en route to Catholic cemeteries evidenced the ineradicable hold of Spain upon the living as well as the dead.

Negros Island, heart of the sugar industry, was agriculturally the wealthiest of the Philippines at the outbreak of war. Endless stretches of silver tasseled cane, the outlines of molasses and alcohol tanks which pierced the even level of cane fields, and warehouses stocked with sugar awaiting shipment to the United States represented the core of the wealth. Success in sugar development had characterized American, British, and Filipino investment on Negros. So interested became the Philippine government that it offered to lend a helping financial hand to keep ever flowing the sweetness from Negros soil.

Along with the chain of crystal filled bags carried to Negros piers was hardwood lumber which had been assembled for export also. In the virgin woodlands of Negros had been discovered untapped resources of high-value building and furniture materials. As a result, the largest hardwood lumber company in the world had opened in Negros forest depths.

A large proportion of the men and women interned in Bacolod depended upon sugar for their livelihood. These people lived upon sugar centrals, independent communities built around a sugar mill. In addition to the houses for staff members, the centrals often included a commissary where staple groceries were for sale, a theater, a hospital with medical staff, golf course, tennis courts, a cold-storage plant of individual lockers, and gardens and orchards which supplied the entire group. Light and water were provided by the central's own power plants. The central built and owned the network of roads and railway lines connecting cane fields with the mill. If there was a water outlet the central built piers. It was a complete, independent world, sufficient unto itself.

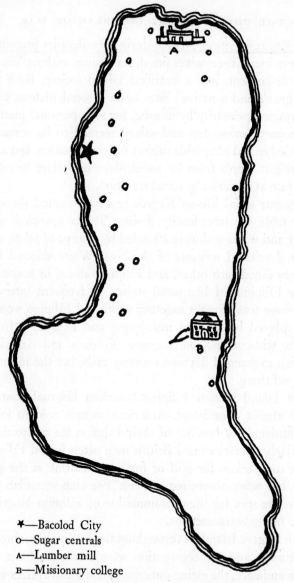

✳—Bacolod City
o—Sugar centrals
A—Lumber mill
B—Missionary college

Map Showing Location of Bacolod City, Producing Sugar Centrals, Lumber Mill, and Missionary College on Negros Island, 1941.

Source: Location of sugar centrals from *Joint Army-Navy Intelligence Service Report* No. 154 (Washington, D.C., 1944), Figure ix, p. 77.

White residents of Negros during the decades preceding the war found themselves fitted, sometimes without knowledge or consent, into a stratified Island society. Both the foreigner's and a native's sites upon a social plateau were determined primarily by income, for such personal matters as property ownership and salary seemed to be common knowledge and acceptable subject for conversation. But anyone might topple from his social plane by failure to maintain face as required by social tradition.

Pre-war social life on Negros revolved around the evening table for inter-family dining. Tables sparkled with silver and wines and were attended by a corps of white uniformed oriental servants of the host. White skinned foreigners dined each other, and Filipinos dined in homes of other Filipinos of like social status. At frequent intervals afternoon teas brought together white and Filipino women who played bridge and mah-jongg and enjoyed refreshments without self-consciousness. Filipino and American women exchanged daytime courtesy calls, but the intimacy stopped there.

By Island custom Filipino-American bisexual contacts were almost nonexistent. American women seldom knew the husbands or families of their Filipino tea companions. Similarly, American and British men often joined Filipino male companions for golf or for a social drink at the golf club, but women were not present. The club verandah was a favorite spot for the consummation of Filipino-American male business transactions.

On Negros Island, as throughout the Philippines, cinema, restaurant, and bus segregation were unknown. Since the show audience, the eating-out crowd, and bus travelers were largely Filipinos, the white patrons took what seats were

TABLE II

Negros Island Centrifugal Sugar Production

Centrals	1940-41 Crop Short tons	Per cent of Philippine total
Negros Island		
1. Bacolod-Murcia Milling Co.	46,045	3.98
2. Binalbagan Estate, Inc.	54,148	4.69
3. Central Azucarera de Bais	50,401	4.36
4. Central Azucarera del Danao	11,931	1.03
5. Central Leonor	3,767	.32
6. Central Palma	9,136	.79
7. Central San Isidro	11,322	.97
8. Hawaiian-Philippine Co.	66,612	5.76
9. Isabela Sugar Co.	35,805	3.10
10. Kabankalan Sugar Co.	13,820	1.20
11. La Carlota Sugar Central	88,636	7.67
12. Lopez Sugar Central Co.	24,303	2.10
13. Ma-ao Sugar Central Co.	49,319	4.27
14. North Negros Sugar Co.	69,060	5.98
15. San Carlos Milling Co.	42,376	3.67
16. San Isidro (De la Rama)		
17. Sta Aniceta (De la Rama)	3,118	.27
18. Talisay-Silay Milling Co.	51,787	4.48
19. Victorias Milling Co.	52,136	4.51
	610,466	59.15

Record crop (1933-34) for Negros was 879,538 short tons, 55.72% of the Philippine total.

Forty-six sugar centrals are listed in the Philippines in 1940-41: 19 on Negros, 16 on Luzon, 6 on Panay, 3 on Mindora, 2 on Leyte.

Source: "Report of the Technical Committee to the President of the Philippines," *American-Philippine Trade Relations*, TC-1 (Washington, D.C., 1944), Table 17, p. 49.

vacant. In contrast to the American theater seating plan, Philippine gallery seats were more expensive than those on the main floor, and white persons attending a movie could most often be found scattered among wealthy Filipinos in the gallery. The purchase of gallery seats was a face saving device. It was generally admitted that the more spacious ground floor was cooler and permitted a better view.

The last pre-war Philippine census, in 1939, showed approximately 51,000 mestizos or mixed bloods in the Islands.[3] These were the offspring of one dark (Filipino) and one light skinned parent. The mestizo is generally the acknowledged scion of a recognized union. In this he is unlike the mulatto in the United States, who seldom has personal contact with his white blood relations and is assumed—unless otherwise proven—to be the offspring of an illegal or clandestine association. The insistence upon legalized marriage by the Filipino is a product of the intense religious training to which Filipinos have been subjected for generations by the Catholic Church. Yet the mestizo has not been fully accepted into the white social life of the Islands.[4]

A term of Philippine duty for American soldiers during and following the Spanish-American war not infrequently culminated in the union of the soldier with a native girl. Soldiers found Filipino girls to be small, neat, slender (the "hipless race" the soldiers called them), and generally attractive by American standards. A private's uniform, which indicated insufficient pay for participation in the white social life, paved the way for an introduction to Filipino girls.

---

[3] Table I, pp. 10-11

[4] An interesting study of attitudes of Filipinos toward other races in the Islands indicated that Filipinos preferred American mestizos to Americans as marriage partners. Serafin E. Macaraig, "Social Attitudes of Filipinos toward Foreigners in the Philippines," *Philippine Social Science Review*, XI (1939), 26-33.

American civilian males who married Filipinos have usually explained their marriages as resulting from the absence of eligible American girls, the unwillingness of fiancées in the States to live in the tropics, or a desire to remain permanently in the Islands. Recognition of the loneliness of the unattached white man in the tropics and the charm of the natives has led British firms to include in their Philippine contracts a statement that marriage within a period ranging up to nine years after leaving the home country invalidates the employment agreement. At the end of five years the young Britisher is brought home for a long vacation and prospective marriage there.

Scattered throughout the Philippines were American women, generally well educated, married to Filipinos. At the outbreak of war several leading Filipino doctors had American wives and on the faculty of the University of the Philippines there had been for many years American teachers who were married to Filipino academicians.

A group unto themselves were the foreign missionaries of the Philippines. They had little in common with the foreign military or the commercial populations. Likewise, Protestant missionaries endeavoring to convert Filipino Catholics had little to share with Island priests whose work was to maintain the Filipino Catholic status quo. Missionary staffs concentrated themselves about mission hospitals and schools, and the nature of their services largely confined their associations and friendships to Filipinos.

The absence in Bacolod (the largest town on Negros) of a place for religious observance by the white Protestant population was an indication of the lack of general religious interest on the part of the non-missionary white residents there. Once, sometimes twice, a year the canon missioner of the Episcopal Church in Manila conducted services for Island white communicants. At such times there was a mass christening of all white Protestant babies born since the missioner's last visit. For Filipinos there were daily Catholic masses in every village.

Sunday for the staffs of the lumber and sugar groups on Negros was an accepted time for all day tiffins. Centered around a midday feast these entertainments began in the morning and lasted through tea in the afternoon. In between periods of eating there was golf for the men and bridge for the women. There was little throughout the orient to unite those who had gone to traffic in foreign souls and those who trafficked in foreign raw materials.

Not only was there racial and economic stratification on Negros, but wherever a handful of one caste gathered together social substratifications resulted. The social and economic ratings on one of the largest sugar centrals on Negros will illustrate this social order:

The manager of the central was social leader as well as chief executive. As such he lived in house number 1, and his telephone number was number 1. In house number 2, telephone number 2, resided the chief engineer. Number 3 house was reserved for the sugar engineer; number 4 for the business manager. In number 5 house was the grounds supervisor; in number 6 the assistant engineer. Number 7 was for the office assistant. These persons were all American or British. Filipino staff houses began with number 8.

In recognition of the rank of the house tenant, the Filipino boy with a daily supply of central garden produce passed from houses 1 to 8 in that order. At each house a selection from the fresh fruits and vegetables was made, the occupants of house number 8 having a choice of what

remained after the seven other households had been satis-
fied. The boy could not follow directly the walkway which
surrounded the central court but must crisscross and re-
trace his steps to insure that no house was served out of
turn. The daily route of the garden boy looked like this:

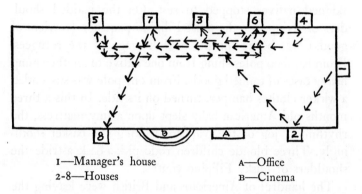

1—Manager's house   A—Office
2-8—Houses   B—Cinema

The intricate societal scheme of Negros, the playing of
roles and the maintaining of face, were original barriers
to the working together of the miscellaneous group within
the Bacolod camp. Internment removed many of these artificial obstructions to human association—at least for the
time being.

3

Opening of the Bacolod Camp

IT WAS June 6, 1942. Halfway down the steep mountain trail the human caravan of 21 white refugees and 35 brown skinned natives stopped to rest. On the padded shoulders of stripped-to-the-waist Filipino paquiaos (carriers of goods) was borne the personal luggage of the refugees. From bamboo poles slung from one native to another hung heavy cases of canned goods. From one pole was suspended a wicker clothes hamper, turned on its side. In this a three months old American baby slept upon a tiny mattress, the rhythmical jog of the paquiaos rocking the basket soothingly. Three blonde children rode pick-a-back astride the shoulders of husky Filipino youths.

The handful of Americans and British were leaving the crude mountain huts in which they had been hiding. They were leaving Binagsukan, "the end of the road," for the uncertainties of a Japanese internment camp. As everything that had been taken into Binagsukan had been carried by human strength, so it must, in part, be moved out again. The Japanese had discovered the mountain hideout. Other little groups of frightened white people were being ferreted out of their hiding places by the invading Japanese. A written order from the Japanese, delivered by a Filipino messenger, demanded that the Binagsukan aliens report to the Bacolod Internment Camp not later than June 10.

Negros Island was one of the last of the Philippines to be occupied by the Japanese, not because of the strong defense of the Island (it was practically defenseless), but because the Japanese had concerned themselves with more strategic military advances in the Islands. Not until May 2 did they land in large number on Negros.

For several months prior to the Japanese landing little groups of Americans and British had secluded themselves deep in the virgin forests of Negros Island. Filipinos and nomadic Negritos who were inhabiting the woodland had brought daily food to the white strangers.

At 3 a.m. on the day of the departure from Binagsukan, kerosene lanterns were burning in every little nipa palm hut, and tiny wood fires were going between the matched stones which supported a pan on the sand-box stoves. Not only breakfast, but also a lunch of fried native bantam chicken, scones, and eggs, was being prepared for the day and a half trip to Bacolod. Water bottles filled, canvas cots folded, and mosquito nets placed conspicuously atop the other luggage, everything was ready for the departure.

Heavily laden white people and natives let themselves down the steep mountain trail with the aid of pointed sticks. Temperature changes were noticeable as they descended from the wooded mountain peak to the sugar-cane fields below. At the far end of the uncut cane was the home of a Filipino hacendero (plantation manager) where the white people were to spend the night en route to Bacolod. Here the natives said good-by before they returned to the hills.

On the morning of Sunday, June 7, the Americans and British piled themselves and a few of their belongings into trucks of the hacendero. They rode standing the last twen-ty-five miles to Bacolod.

On all the public schoolhouses, on country stores, and often on telephone poles and trees along the roadway were posters placed by the Japanese. The most popular was a handclasp labeled: "Let's work for peace—Japan and the Philippines." Another poster, "The New Philippines," showed school children at their desks. They were Filipino children with a strange, slant-eyed look on their faces. The Filipinos that the white people passed looked at them without expression, not daring to wave, yet showing none of the animosity toward the Americans that the Japanese were anxious to foster.

The Americans and British passed near the sugar central from which they had fled to Binagsukan. The smoke blackened concrete walls of the sugar mill were still standing. There was only rubbish where the houses of the people in the trucks had formerly been. A few heat-distorted bed springs, glued to the parched grass by a heavy film of molasses which had escaped from the burning sugar warehouse, were all that remained of "home." Former residents of the central closed their eyes to shut out the scene of devastation.

At the gateway to another sugar central, on the outskirts of Bacolod, the Americans and British met a Japanese sentinel who ordered them to stop by raising his gun. The sentinel stood below a sign in incorrect English, "Please bow the guard." They bowed the guard, as requested. After scrutinizing the summons to Bacolod, the guard allowed the "enemy aliens"—that was the wording on the summons—to pass.

The trucks slowed down at the entrance to the Bacolod North Elementary School, its grounds enclosed by a high barbed wire fence. Here all Negros civilian aliens were to be interned. Japanese soldiers quartered in the school principal's former home, directly across from the main school building, instructed the new arrivals to enter the grounds, to go to the small home economics building there, and await further orders. This being Sunday, they were told, the High Command might not like being bothered! The High Command was spending the day playing golf at the Bacolod Country Club—where the aliens themselves had spent their Sundays before the arrival of the Japanese in the Philippines.

The men, women, and children entered the three-room home economics building and discovered enough chairs for about half their number. Those who had no chair sat outside on the hot concrete steps in the morning sun. It was now eleven o'clock. In looking about the small building they discovered an old stove, water faucets which did not run, and a toilet which did not flush.

From 11 a.m. to 3:30 p.m. they sat, stood, and perspired in the heat, waiting for someone to tell them what to do. Hundreds of flies appeared, stung their faces and hands, and clung to them. The children, uncomfortable and crying, begged for a place to lie down, but the adults did not dare get a mat from the trucks until the Japanese had inspected their luggage and given authority to open it.

When the Japanese High Command arrived, the Americans and British lined up for their first roll call. The Japanese told them that three elementary school classrooms had been assigned to the group of twenty-one internees, that the men were to sleep together in one of these rooms and the women and children to divide the other two rooms between them. The Japanese said nothing to the internees about food, though the internees thought, of course, that provisions for feeding them had been made. Just as a precaution, however, they had brought along with them, on the truck, a small miscellaneous supply of canned goods, and milk concentrates for the children.

As soon as they left the home economics building to go to their sleeping quarters in the U-shaped classroom building, the new arrivals met twenty-five internees who had reported a day before them. The Binagsukan people had seen no white faces except those in their own group since their flight to the mountains, and these other people had been as securely cut off on another part of the Island. There was such joy in the reunion of old friends that all worries were overlooked for the moment. The internees who had arrived first, however, soon disclosed what they had discovered about their new home.

There were no cooking facilities; the only usable toilets were out of doors. There were no bathing facilities whatsoever. Until the camp could get organized and build stoves and eating sheds, each individual would have to prepare and eat his own food in whatever manner he was able. Sticks picked up from the ground would have to serve for fuel.

Anxiously the recent arrivals had their first look at their new quarters. What filth! The walls were dark with dirt, and heavy with cobwebs. Large, black roaches scuttled into the corners, and the place smelled of the human refuse which had dried upon the floor.

Evidently these were the first white prisoners that the Japanese soldiers in Bacolod had seen. The second night of the camp was marked by five Japanese inspections after the internees had gone to bed. The first inspection was at 10 p.m. A soldier flashed on the lights as he and a half-dozen of his comrades peered into each mosquito net to see what their new prisoners looked like. At midnight, at 2, at 3, and at 4 a.m. these same Japanese and other guards walked into the open doors of the internees' rooms (the internees had been told that the doors of their rooms were never to be closed) and again turned on the lights and again scrutinized the sleepy, pale faces.

The next morning, fresh meat, vegetables, fruit, and bread were sent to the internees by friendly Filipinos in Bacolod. These gifts the Japanese permitted to enter, though the bearers of the foodstuffs were stopped at the camp gate. The internees could not communicate with anyone on the outside, nor could they receive or send written messages. Later, they were told, a few visitors would be permitted into camp to talk with internees, one at a time, in the presence of a Japanese interpreter. Arrangements might be made for letter communication at some future time.

The internee group grew until there was a total of 148 men, women, and children, ranging in age from three months to 80 years. They were of American, British, Dutch, Filipino, Spanish, and Italian nationality. Racially they were of Caucasian, Negroid, Indian, and Malayan extraction.

Nationality gave little clue to the racial or social heritage of the internees. Americans included not only white, long-time residents of the United States, but American Indians and a Negro. Nationalized Americans were of Spanish, Chinese, Swiss, and Scandinavian birth. American citizenship was also claimed by Filipino wives and mestizo descendants of American men. An Hawaiian-American family claimed nationality through American male heritage.

British nationals varied also in color and in background. They were Englishmen, Australians, and Scots and their marriage ties had extended British citizenship to dark women and shaded offspring. The Dutch in camp were all priests, and the order of celibacy proscribed their bringing with them the colorful dependents claimed by other national groups. One of the interned Filipino nationals was an American lawyer who had taken out Filipino nationality as an aid in the Island practice of his profession.

The Japanese were completely confused by the status of women and children of international marriages. Some Filipino wives of American men were considered Philippine citizens. Other Filipino wives were assumed to have taken the nationality of American husbands. Mestizo children were often assigned nationality by color of skin rather than known national heritage. The light mestizo offspring of an American were more likely to be interned than his dark ones. American women married to Filipinos were at first interned as American citizens. Later they were released as Philippine nationals.

When a young American woman married to a Spaniard was brought to camp and her three small children were forced to remain outside with their father, the commandant was asked how nationality of the children had been determined. In this case, he stated, the children had been born to the neutrality of their father but the wife had not changed her nationality by marriage.

At its beginning the Bacolod group was predominantly Catholic, but the arrival of the missionary staff of a Presbyterian college evened the Protestant-Catholic ratio. The three American Indians were a clear-cut religious minority in their daily observance of a modified sun worship.

Educationally the internees ranged from trained professionals—a doctor, a lawyer, college teachers—to illiterates.

TABLE III

Age, Sex, and Nationality Distribution of All Bacolod Internees, 1942-43

	TOTAL		Amer.		Brit.		Dutch		Filip.		Span.		Ital.	
	M	F	M	F	M	F	M	F	M	F	M	F	M	F
TOTAL	83	65	53	33	18	21	4		4	6	2	2	2	3
Under 1 yr.	4	2	1	1	1	1			1		1			
1-10 yrs.	8	10	4	6	2	2					1	1	1	1
11-20 yrs.		4		1		2								1
21-30 yrs.	1	10		5		2			1	2	1			
31-40 yrs.	14	14	7	8	3	4	3		1	1				1
41-50 yrs.	22	20	12	11	7	7	1		1	2			1	
51-60 yrs.	20	5	15	1	5	3			1					
61-70 yrs.	12		12											
71-80 yrs.	2		2											

SUMMARY OF TABLE III

	TOTAL	AMER.	BRIT.	DUTCH	FILIP.	SPAN.	ITAL.
TOTAL	148	86	39	4	10	4	5
Men	71	48	15	4	3		1
Women	49	25	16		6	1	1
Children:							
Under 11	24	12	6		1	3	2
11-20 yrs.	4	1	2				1

Socio-economically they were distributed between high-salaried and profit-sharing corporation executives and beachcombers.

Internees had but one common trait. They were all "enemy aliens." The earliest Bacolod internees arrived in June, 1942 and the last in January, 1943. Most of these were in the camp when it was closed (on one hour's notice) on March 2, 1943. On that date the Bacolod internees boarded

TABLE IV

*Adult Bacolod Internees by Occupation and Sex,
December, 1941**

	TOTAL		Amer.		Brit.		Dutch		Filip.		Span.		Ital.	
	M	F	M	F	M	F	M	F	M	F	M	F	M	F
TOTAL	71	49	48	25	15	16	4		3	6	1	1	1	
Sugar central executives	21		17		4									
Other central employees	7		5		2									
Lumber mill executives	5		3		2									
Other lumber employees	11		10		1									
Doctors	1		1											
Lawyers	1								1					
Teachers	2	1	2	1										
Protestant missionaries	2	7	2	6		1								
Catholic priests & nuns	7	2	2	2	1			4						
Other employed	10	1	4	1	4				1				1	
Non-employed	4	38	2	15	1	15			1	6	1			1

* 21 years and older.

a Japanese ship for transfer to Manila. Due to the temporary internment of some and the late internment of others, the age and sex distribution of Bacolod internees varied at different times. Males always exceeded females, however, and children accounted for never less than fifteen per cent of the total.

When three Filipino wives of American men were released in December, 1942, the commandant was asked for an explanation. He advised internees, "We cannot have too many Filipinos—pure or half caste—in this camp. The only reason for interning Americans, British, and Dutch on Negros Island is to protect you from the Filipinos who might harm you." This statement, after the years of harmony between the white foreigners and the natives of Negros, caused surprise.

It was true, however, that at least two plantation owners brought into camp found protection in internment. Filipino tenants and laborers who had long been victims of a sugar plantation peonage system not unlike the United States cotton share cropper plan at its worst (whereby the tenant never gets out of debt to his landlord) had taken advantage of the general upheaval of war to murder landlords against whom they had long held a grievance. Two internee plantation owners had been threatened.

The interned American Negro was the first that many had seen. Finding him unlike the Filipinos with whom they had been raised, interned American children were particularly excited by his arrival. The Negro had been forcibly taken from his Filipino wife and eight children and brought to Bacolod from one of the sugar mills.

Twenty-two men and women were rounded up at Dumaguete on the eastern side of Negros and brought to Bacolod by boat. Normally an eight hour overland drive, the war-time boat trip between the two towns required three days. Filipino guerrillas had destroyed overland bridges and the water route was the only one which remained open. On the sea trip men and women were placed upon the decks of a small vessel and when it rained they crawled into the holds for shelter. There were no toilets, and no food was provided for the trip by the Japanese.

The Japanese showed no respect for the robe. Catholic priests (American, British, Dutch) were picked up about the Island. Two nuns from the staff of a sugar central hospital were brought to camp with nothing but a change of habit each.

There was general distress when a mestizo family brought bed bugs into camp with them. The father had served in the American Navy during World War I, and though he was not an American citizen he had evidenced to the Japanese sufficient sympathy toward the United States to justify his imprisonment.

"Undesirable" and "desirable" individuals were scattered indiscriminately throughout the crowded quarters. There was hardly a room which did not have at least one whose failure to bathe or whose snoring did not annoy other internees, but there was no attempt to segregate either by race or personality traits. As new internees arrived they fitted themselves into unoccupied rooms or into vacant bed spaces in partially filled quarters.

Women were less tolerant than men of an undesirable member of their sex. Shrewd scheming followed suspicions of the women that one internee was meeting the husband of another in secret rendezvous after dark. In the interests of the general well-being and maintenance of order in the community, the situation was regarded with concern.

In whispered conferences it was decided to point out to the commandant that the woman in question had entered the camp under a false claim of nationality. No moral issue was raised with the commandant; the women felt capable of handling that angle of the case themselves. Because of her nationality, the woman was later released.

Of the 148 men, women, and children interned in Bacolod, 37 were of dark blood, pure or mixed. These were the Filipino wives and the mestizo children of internees; they were the part Chinese, part Hawaiian, part Portuguese men, women, and children. They also included the Indians and the Negro. Yet a few of these called themselves white and had been accepted into white social groups. It was a common occurrence in the Islands for an almost white Filipino mestizo to claim Spanish blood and denounce his Filipino heritage in a final step toward absorption into the alien civilization of the Islands.

In addition to those who were themselves of colored extraction there were twenty-three white men who had lived, prior to the war, with Filipino wives or mistresses.

There were four interned white women who were married to uninterned Filipino men. Only 57 per cent—slightly more than half—of the internees were all-white, that is, related by neither inheritance nor marriage association to dark skinned peoples. Being closely confined in such a mixed community was difficult for a few of the most racially exclusive of pre-war Island society. Their touch-me-not attitude made early internment unnecessarily unpleasant for themselves as well as for the racially mixed. For the latter seemed no less displeased by the compulsory association.

Widely discussed within the camp were the efforts of one family to conceal evidence of racial mixture. The story was told that the parents had enrolled their child in a racially exclusive school on Mindanao. This school required full Caucasian inheritance for admission. It was rumored that after acceptance of the application by the school an anonymous note from neighbors gave details of the unsuspected racial history. The school application was cancelled.

The parents of the child and the sender of the note which was apparently the cause of cancelling the school enrollment were interned together. Three years of close human relations, previously untried, between black, brown, and white necessarily resulted in a re-evaluation of racial and cultural differences.

4

Bacolod Camp Organization: The Pooling of Food Supplies

HARDLY was the camp gate closed behind the first groups of internees when they initiated the internee organization and program which were adopted by later arrivals. In this chapter and the next two chapters are described the internee policy concerning the equalization of private property, and the camp plan of work, health, recreation, religion, and communication.

The Bacolod North Elementary School was situated about a mile from Bacolod on a dirt road off the paved highway. It consisted of a nineteen-room classroom unit, a separate home economics laboratory and manual training shop, two outdoor toilets, and a storage shed.

School grounds covered approximately five acres and were enclosed in a six foot high barbed-wire fence. Still attached to the wires was a high voltage electrical mechanism installed by Filipinos who had interned Negros Island Japanese nationals in the school during the early months of the war before the Japanese Army occupied the Island. A single large wire gate afforded entrance to the grounds.

The main building, U-shaped, contained seven classrooms on each wing and three rooms and two smaller offices faced a vine covered front verandah. The rooms on the wings also opened on long, narrow porches. Electricity lighted the buildings; water was drawn from faucets housed in the outdoor toilets.

The home economics laboratory and the manual training shop lay south of the main building, and like it were almost bare of furnishings. Scattered, small sized desks and sawali screens (made of native woven fiber) found about the grounds and in the buildings came to be valued for the construction materials they provided rather than for present utility.

Cots and beds brought by the first two groups of internees filled six of the seven rooms on the north school-room wing. In compliance with the Japanese sex segregation order men placed their bedding in some rooms, women in others. By internee arrangement husbands and wives slept in adjacent quarters and babies and small children were segregated at the end of the wing. The seventh room, internees left vacant for adult recreation and as a children's play room on rainy days. Later arrivals filled all the south wing and one of the front rooms. The rooms averaged ten internees each. Two front classrooms became the office and sleeping quarters of the Japanese commandant. The two remaining small front offices were used as a camp library and a supply room.

The second evening of internment the group of men, women, and children gathered on the back steps of the sleeping quarters. They sat in the twilight uncertain as to what they might expect from the Japanese or from their own group. The Japanese had not fed them and as yet had made no arrangements for future provision of food.

A middle-aged Scotsman, manager of a large hardwood lumber company on Negros, arose. "Some of us have brought much to camp," he said, "others nothing. The latter came empty-handed through no fault of their own. They were hustled away from their homes and hiding places by the Japanese with only an overnight bag. It is my

Chart of Bacolod Civilian Internment Camp

(North Bacolod Elementary School)

A—School building which housed internees and commandant
B—Hospital (former home economics laboratory)
C—Kitchen and dining room (manual training shop)
D—Men's toilet
E—Women's toilet
F—Showers (constructed by internees)
G—Storage shed   I—Pasture for camp livestock
H—Gardens   J—Japanese guard houses

suggestion that those who have brought food to camp share with others. I propose that all personal food supplies go into a camp storage place for equal use of all internees."

There had already been murmurings among some of the mothers that they feared for the immediate health of babies and children for whom they had brought no milk. It was known generally that the Scotsman who had suggested communal food division was himself the owner of more than twenty cases of evaporated and powdered milk. In addition he had brought case lots of preserved meats, vegetables, fruit, and sacks of rice and camotes. He had the largest personal food reserve in the camp. Other internees had brought smaller quantities of similar items.

A woman addressed the Scotsman, "What about those of us who have brought food? We have paid cash for these goods or have been charged for them. Will we be given credit for what we contribute to the camp?"

The Scotsman replied, "I think no individual inventory of goods contributed should be made. No credit should be given anyone for his contributions. I think each should contribute all that he now has or is able to secure later, without thought of remuneration."

A motion that the Scotsman's suggestion be adopted as a camp policy received an undisputed internee vote. A second motion that the Scotsman be elected internee director of the camp was also undisputed. In the capacity of director he would preside at internee meetings and represent the camp in its contacts with the Japanese. Thus ended the first of many camp councils. The early meetings were all symphonies of complete accord. But with increasing numbers and variety in camp personnel came disharmony in the administration of internee affairs.

From the first there were two distinct aspects of the social control of the Bacolod camp: (1) Japanese regulations and (2) internee policies. The former were rules passed from the commandant to the internees through the voice of the director. Such orders limited internee movements to camp boundaries, and restricted communication with the outside. They prescribed cleanliness of grounds and quarters, and demanded recognition, by bowing, of the dominant position of the Japanese. Within the limits of these regulations internees worked out their own policy with regard to food, work, health, and recreation. Internee decisions were arrived at by a majority vote of the adult population.

To assist him in his administrative duties the director selected eight men as advisers. These men were chosen from sugar central staffs, missionaries and priests, and the different racial groups, but they had no authority. When matters of internee policy arose they cast individual votes.

Early conversations with the commandant indicated no provisions for feeding internees, and information from him concerning future prospects for aid was not forthcoming. On the third day, in accordance with the newly decided internee policy, canned goods were removed from sleeping quarters and stored in the school shed. A cooking staff was organized to draw upon these supplies and serve them sparingly, but equally, to the camp.

The first week friendly Filipinos came daily to the gate with gifts of native vegetables, meat, fruit, and bread. An American woman, experienced in managing an Island boarding home for foreigners, assumed charge of the preparation of meals on a camp-wide basis. A crude outdoor stove took shape as a result of internee labor. Over it was raised a sawali protection from sun and rain. Individual cooking utensils were donated to the camp and a few larger ones were bought from Bacolod merchants through (but not by) the Japanese.

Women worked in daily shifts of kitchen duty, preparing and serving the food out of doors. On rainy days internees took their food to sleeping quarters. At other times they ate upon the grass. It was only after a month of insistent requests from the camp director that the Japanese consented to turn over to internees the manual training shop for their use as a combined kitchen and dining room.

Filipino food gifts tapered off, then ceased, as outside living conditions and Japanese regulations became more stringent. The discovery of a permanent basis for securing regular food supplies was the consuming search of internees. The Japanese still offered no hint of assistance. Internee discussion eventually revealed a possible temporary source of food when the director offered the use of his personal and company funds for the purchase of camp supplies. This money had been left in Bacolod with neutral Swiss. Internees were to sign legal notes promising repayment to the director after the war for their pro-rata share of these expenditures.

With the permission of the Japanese the director arranged with the Swiss to send small daily supplies of food and fuel to the camp until his funds were exhausted.

Arrangements were made in the presence of the Japanese commandant who expressed no objection to internees using their own money for foodstuffs. The commandant asked how much money there was in camp but received an evasive answer, for no inventory had been taken. Five hundred pèsos had been removed by a Japanese guard from one internee when he was searched upon his arrival but funds of others had been unmolested.

Rice, corn, camotes, dried fish were bought with the director's money. Also garden tools and seeds, medical supplies, carabao milk, and coconuts. Piles of rough hewn logs for kitchen fuel were accumulated. Live pigs, sheep, rabbits, chickens, ducks, and a young carabao were purchased for future consumption, the livestock in the meantime to share the crowded school grounds with internees. Japanese who watched internees frantically stock their larder made no comment. The doubling, trebling, quadrupling of food prices did not hinder internees' buying, for they felt that any day the money would run out or the Japanese might cut off this outside source.

The Swiss buyer for the camp reported to the director (again in the presence of the commandant) when the director's funds were exhausted. Credit buying was then attempted but became impossible as Bacolod supplies were depleted and merchants felt the pressure upon themselves for cash.

The commandant was asked repeatedly when the Japanese would assume responsibility for providing food and fuel for their prisoners. There was no satisfactory reply. Efforts to reach the ear of Japanese authorities higher than the commandant had been unsuccessful. In August, however, two months after internment, Colonel Ota, the commanding officer of the Japanese Army on Negros came to camp to discuss the food situation with internees. During his visit he made no food commitments; but he distributed a free cigarette to each internee woman, spoke optimistically of the near ending of the war in Japan's favor, and bade internees to carry on in the spirit of Bushido. Three weeks later the colonel came back to continue his cheery destructiveness of internee hopes and to say that he was being transferred from Negros. Expectation of aid from the Japanese vanished.

For eight months internees consumed in meager proportion and with little enjoyment the food supplies which they had accumulated. Concentration upon gardening so expanded that space for outdoor recreation and for livestock was abandoned in favor of garden production.

The rice supply and the garden, it was soon recognized, would ultimately determine just how long internees would be able to carry on as suggested by Colonel Ota. Camp animals were slaughtered rapidly when inadequate feed and shelter for them resulted in numerous livestock deaths. Long periods without meat were followed by days of too much in an effort to consume carcasses before spoilage.

Fear concerning the possible duration of internment was increased by the continued refusal of the Japanese to take over responsibility for internee welfare. The gradual depletion of irreplaceable food resources left internees in a state of near panic and they set aside the remaining canned goods as uncertain protection against a terrifying future.

Finally, in January, the eighth month of imprisonment, Colonel Ota's successor paid his first visit to the camp. The new colonel inspected the camp garden and the remainder of the camp-owned canned goods. The latter were then being drawn upon for the internee sick only. After a hasty tour of the camp the colonel made the following relevant and irrelevant comments: 1. The Bacolod camp had a good reputation for behavior, there having been no serious trouble there; 2. Should trouble arise in the camp the director would be held personally responsible; 3. The food shortage of which internees spoke and the request for funds for support of the camp would be considered later; 4. A look at the camp worm-infested rice supply, which internees said was beyond salvage, showed this rice to be no worse than that eaten by Japanese soldiers. The colonel's attitude seemed to be that internees should continue to look after themselves.

During the months of effort on the part of the director to have the Japanese assume responsibility for feeding internees, the camp was slowly dividing itself into two antagonistic groups. The issues were all related to food: whether internee private funds should be commandeered for group food supplies; whether individual purchases and gifts of food should be forbidden; whether the remaining canned goods should be consumed at once or conserved for a later emergency.

An appeal had been made by the director for internee cash contributions for additional camp supplies. A few men and women responded. No one as yet knew how much money there was in camp, though it was generally believed that one or two individuals were withholding large sums. Certain internees who had contributed canned goods to the camp felt that the claims upon personal property should cease there. Cash, they said, should remain a private possession. Others disagreed.

A corollary to the suggestion that private funds become public funds was the suggestion that the spending of private funds be restricted. At the time this discussion took place those with cash could buy fruit, eggs, and sweets through the guards. Prices charged by the Japanese who acted as go-between for merchants and internees were often known to be ten times those paid by the guards for food in Bacolod. The ability of internees to pay these prices, it was argued within the camp, fortified the belief of the Japanese that internees needed no aid from the Japanese. The seeming affluence of a few internees was causing the slow starvation of the larger group, it was contended.

The beginning of the ill feeling over food could be traced to the first months of camp. When the early arrivals voted to pool their personal supplies of food and to share these with future as well as present internees, they did not realize that this generous move would stop almost altogether the bringing into camp, for camp use, other personally owned foodstuffs. The report of the pooling decision spread over Negros. Unfortunately for the camp, some of the later internees (known to have well stocked home larders and opportunity of transporting goods to camp) arrived empty handed. They left their canned goods with outside relatives or Filipino friends who were to send the food periodically as personal gifts which the camp could not touch. Such actions caused the milk of human kindness to sour in some internee breasts.

Dissension over the rate and method of utilization of the camp supply of canned goods resulted in a crisis in the kitchen. Charges were made that the manager of the kitchen staff was depleting canned foods too rapidly. She was accused of inadequate knowledge concerning the use of native vegetables and meat available in the camp grounds. A former home economics teacher of Filipino children seemed to have the needed qualifications, for she knew native food habits and native methods of preparation. Under her management the kitchen functioned on a "Save the canned goods!" motto.

Opposition to the above kitchen policy was led by an interned doctor. In December he requested that one teaspoon of tinned butter be given daily (as long as it lasted) to the children, who were losing weight rapidly. He emphasized the seriousness of camp dietary deficiencies, and at the same time he asked for daily limited quantities of milk for all internees until the milk was exhausted. These requests went before a committee of men and women who had been elected for the purpose of allocating canned goods to the kitchen and the hospital. The request for butter was refused but milk was added to the breakfast coffee for adults.

The doctor headed a steadily enlarging group who believed that the present health conditions of internees did not justify the withholding of vital canned goods longer. The camp director, on the other hand, led those who felt that a still greater emergency lay ahead. Admittedly the camp diet was inadequate. Rice which had been bought was now old and moldy. Vegetables from the garden provided but two or three meals for the entire group in a week's time. Meat twice a week was a rarity. The sugar supply was exhausted. Coffee was but lightly colored water. The small canned supplies assumed the unnatural proportions of a food mirage to hungry men and women.

Fear of confiscation of remaining canned foods by the Japanese abetted the efforts of the doctor, for he said that unless the food were eaten it might be lost to the Japanese. On January 10 the Japanese supplied a basis for these fears when they went into the storage shed and checked supplies there.

Hardly had the Japanese left the storage quarters when the director called for volunteers to arrange for a distribution of the stored foodstuffs to individuals. After sorting the supplies the goods were distributed as follows: To all adults—2 cans soup, 2 cans fruit juice, 2 cans beans, 2 cans beef, 1/4 pound butter, 1 pound Klim; additional for babies and children—1 tin cocoa, 1 Ovaltine, 1 oatmeal, 1 peanut butter, 1 dried fruit, 1 tin crackers, 1 honey or syrup, and 1 case evaporated milk. The remainder of the canned goods was re-boxed and assigned five cases to each room. These quantities of food seemed large to internees, but in reality they would provide sufficient nutriment for the total camp population for one week only. Many of the cases assigned for storage in the rooms held fruit juices which would be invaluable in the treatment of tropical fevers and other illnesses, but were of little general nutritive value.

It was emphasized by the director that the distributed foodstuffs were still *camp* supplies. These individual rations were to be held available for an emergency. However, such an emergency was to be determined by the camp and was not to be a matter for individual discretion. Rumor was rife in the camp at this time that the Japanese were planning to abandon the Bacolod site and move internees to another place. The emergency for which the canned goods were to be conserved would be such a move as this if it materialized, or any other situation whereby internees were separated from their garden produce. Uncertain as the present was, to the director the future looked darker.

Transference of the food from a locked supply shed to the personal care of hungry men and women had one of the following three results: (1) pilfering of the supplies; (2) determination to starve before violation of the trust of holding the food; or (3) alignment with a fast developing movement to destroy, by proper legislative methods, camp control over the food.

The wide extent of pilfering was not known until the subsequent check of supplies aboard the S.S. *Naga,* when the long awaited emergency was at hand. Between the pilferers and those who endorsed and carried out the public ownership scheme there emerged a strong group in favor of reopening for public discussion and vote the entire food policy. The original general enthusiasm for sharing and its resultant camp solidarity no longer existed.

On February 22 the director called the internees together to discuss the food situation. He explained the impossibility of securing additional supplies from the outside because of the lack of money or credit. The heavy drain upon the camp garden and the exhaustion of camp livestock were again pointed out. Appeals for food from the Japanese had continued to bring no response. A letter to the International Red Cross, calling attention to the plight of internees and asking for aid, had been handed to the commandant for posting but there had been no reply.

The director proposed two alternatives for the camp, both of which called for curtailed use of available foods. He suggested, first, serving two meals a day instead of three. If this were not acceptable to internees, he suggested a one-third reduction in the daily allowance of food, the smaller amount to be served at the usual hours. The director suggested that canned goods, except for the sick, be held until all other foods were exhausted. The plan of the director called for further tightening of internee belts and a grim determination to see through the internment experience in unity.

A motion was made that the director's plan of reduced consumption be adopted. In the discussion which followed, the plan was bitterly denounced. To demand hunger and possible further ill health of internees while canned goods remained in their care was characterized by some internees as inexcusable and inhuman. The camp seemed about equally balanced in the weighing of the future against the present. After eight months of cooperative endeavor and endurance the camp was on the verge of an irrevocable split.

The meeting called by the director was held after the six o'clock roll call, and the nine o'clock curfew would necessitate its adjournment. As the curfew hour drew near the opposition moved that the motion for curtailed food be tabled. The tabling measure carried and the meeting was adjourned for one week.

During the following days internees talked of little except the food situation. They were either strongly for or strongly against the director. In pre-conference sessions they pledged their votes for the coming public meeting. But the session was never held.

On the morning of February 28, the day before that set for the food conference, a black sedan marked Bacolod Taxi Company brought a Japanese officer to the camp. At a signal from him the Filipino driver opened wide the car doors and took out baskets of fresh food which he dumped upon the ground. There were hundreds of leeks and small tomatoes, two sacks of camotes, two hundred fifty bantam eggs, and two sacks of dried fish. Consternation was on the faces of internees who were peering from behind front verandah vines and out of doorways. Here was the first food that the Japanese had sent to the camp since the "enemy aliens" had been confined there almost nine months before. Some men and women had prayed for manna from heaven but they did not expect it to be delivered by the Japanese in a taxi.

The Japanese officer brought amazing news. He said the Japanese had decided to pay the camp a twenty-five cents per person per day food allowance, retroactive to November. He had with him this allowance for the months of November and December. The foodstuffs he had brought had been deducted from this cash, as had been light and water used by the camp for nine months, June through February. There was little of the allowance remaining. However, this strange system of bookkeeping did not concern internees at the moment. There was too great happiness in the knowledge that the Japanese had at last assumed some responsibility for feeding the camp.

There were no further internee meetings. Two days later, on the afternoon of March 2, after one hour's notice, men, women, and children were placed aboard a ship for Manila.

5

Bacolod Camp Organization:
Work and Health

BY JAPANESE regulation internees were to keep the grounds and camp quarters clean. Otherwise there were no instructions regarding work. The organization of a labor program, the assignment of duties, and the enforcement of work rules were left to the internees themselves.

Certain essential duties were immediately apparent: gardening, carpentry, garbage disposal, toilet sanitation, preparation of food, as well as care of grounds and quarters. Certain types of work were more desirable than others, but equitable distribution of labor assignments was sought by a system of rotation. Least pleasant of the men's jobs were garbage disposal, sanitation, and cleaning of the commandant's office—the latter a care-of-quarters duty. With the exception of dishwashing, all camp domestic duties and the care of the sick became the responsibility of women.

The camp labor policy depended for its success entirely upon its altruistic appeal and internee recognition of joint responsibility. Each individual was assigned his share of chores. There were no perquisites for difficult or overtime jobs. The sole reward for constructive effort was a betterment of camp circumstances.

Special, sedentary tasks went to the elderly and sick. A chronic sprue sufferer sharpened kitchen knives, razor blades and scissors in his room. A retired woman missionary, unable to stand kitchen duties, gave music lessons to interned children. Hair cutting and the replacement of broken cot or bed parts were also within the camp program. Fees were neither charged nor expected for services exchanged within the camp.

As a whole the internees worked hard and long. Two outdoor showers—roofless walls enclosing a water extension from the toilet faucets—were the construction of amateur carpenters and plumbers. A water line was extended from the outdoor toilets to the camp kitchen. Sinks for the new kitchen were hand hammered from roofing tin, and school benches found within the camp were converted into dining tables and seats. Arrivals in Bacolod in early June knew that the stifling days and nights would soon be followed by incessant rains and that the dilapidated coverings of the toilets must be patched before the downpours came.

Special jobs were announced by a call for volunteers to report from the work upon which they were engaged. Volunteer labor stoned dogs and slaughtered and butchered camp animals. Regular volunteer activities in addition to assigned duties were not uncommon. An example of such activities was the work of a gray haired woman. She sorted and catalogued books she found in the school and other books brought in by internees. She opened a camp library. She taught bilingual (Spanish-American) classes for internee children and prepared handbooks for their use. Late in the afternoon, after the cooks had left the kitchen, she roasted green coffee for the next day's breakfast. These activities she timed so that they did not interfere with her regular camp assignments.

Only once was there open rebellion against camp duties. A former executive defied any internee to make him work. When he refused to report to jobs assigned him, however, he was ignored by other internees. They took over his duties without delay or comment. The failure of his actions to disrupt the camp schedule or to attract attention to himself resulted in his somewhat sheepishly returning to his assigned tasks.

The camp had been opened but a short time when the unsanitary surroundings and drastic changes in routine and in diet showed effect in numerous illnesses. At the end of the first two weeks there were five serious cases of dysentery. There was one interned doctor but he had been given half-hour notice to leave his Negros hospital and had not been permitted to bring medical supplies with him. Individual internee medicines were pooled but these failed to provide little except iodine, mercurochrome, aspirin and mild aperients.

In response to the director's request for medicines the Japanese sent one of their own doctors to visit the camp patients. This doctor brought with him a few medical supplies—Japanese ones—which the internee doctor refused to administer since he was unacquainted with them. The internee doctor asked for American pharmaceuticals which he knew were obtainable on the Island. The Japanese doctor replied: "If you refuse Japanese supplies you yourselves will suffer. But if you will pay me in advance I may be able to secure for you a few American-made medicines. I shall send you the prices for these and you can decide whether you wish me to make the purchases for you." When the prices came they were staggering, but individual internees bought.

Sick men, women, and children were housed with well ones. To prevent a camp-wide epidemic of dysentery, permission to use the home economics building as a hospital was secured from the commandant. Though the home economics building consisted of three rooms and a bath, the Japanese limited one room to the use of sick internees. Internees were forbidden to enter the front room but another similar to the one for the sick was converted into a hospital kitchen.

The hospital building contained no beds, and, as no extra ones were available, patient and bed were transferred simultaneously to the hospital. The hospitalized also provided their own linens, gowns, soap, towels, toilet paper, and medical supplies. Families and friends of early patients looked after their needs, but this resulted in confusion and inadequate care. A nursing staff was organized, headed by two nuns with former Negros hospital experience.

From the time of his internment the American doctor was in disfavor with the Japanese. His insistence that he be allowed to bring to the camp medicines from his hospital had resulted in his being beaten and kicked by the Japanese. His ability to serve sick internees was limited by the refusal of the commandant to provide him with medicines or give him permission for their purchase.

The commandant advised the director that he would send to the camp, upon internee request, a Filipino doctor in Japanese employ. This doctor was frequently consulted by internees, not because of faith in his ability as a practitioner, but because of his ability to procure and resell medicines securable in no other way.

Intestinal and kidney disorders and tropical fevers were responsible for the greatest number of hospital cases. Among the sickest of the internees was a tubercular missionary brought in upon a stretcher. Sprue, gallstones and leg ulcers required long hospitalization of other men and women. In each case of serious illness the commandant volunteered to move the patient to the Japanese Army hospital in Bacolod. With the exception of two transfers—in both cases where death was inevitable—the offers were not accepted.

The camp policy with regard to health necessitated special distribution of both food and services, and, since the food supply was held in common ownership, a camp decision was necessary before special supplies could be diverted to a sick individual or to a group. Canned milk, fruit juices, cereals, were allocated to the hospital. Bananas, when obtainable, went to the sprue patients. The finest produce from the garden and choicest cuts of camp meats supplied the hospital kitchen. Though services in the hospital were longer in hours and often more strenuous than other work assignments, there was at no time a shortage of volunteer assistants for the nuns in charge of nursing the sick.

Accidents were frequent. Following is the hospital experience of an injured child which typifies the cooperation and the confusion in affairs of health:

A scream from a two year old boy playing outside the open-top shower while his mother bathed within brought an internee from the garden to his side. Blood was gushing from the child's foot, which was nailed to the ground with the pointed end of a garbage pick-up stick rammed through from above. The internee extracted the iron peg and carried the boy to the hospital. There was no doubt of the seriousness of the wound. The commandant was asked by the nuns in charge of the hospital to call Japanese headquarters at once for anti-tetanus serum. The iron which had pierced the child's foot was filthy with garbage and rust.

Awaiting a reply from the Japanese the nuns forced iodine through the wound by inserting an eye dropper in one of the openings.

The Filipino doctor sent by the Japanese came to camp four hours later without the serum. The child's parent must pay in advance for it. The doctor would do a special favor by securing a vial of 5,000 units from a friend. The child needed only 1,500 units of serum, but the entire vial must be bought. The price was P25.00 ($12.50), old Philippine currency.

The parent had only "emergency money" printed on Negros after the outbreak of war when transportation between the Islands had been stopped. Philippine President Quezon had authorized the issuance of these special war notes; still they were of questionable value.

A fellow internee quickly brought money for the serum, a personal loan to the parent. The doctor was urged not to delay longer. The following day, 36 hours after the injury, the anti-tetanus serum was administered in the arm, 1,500 units. Two days later the Filipino doctor returned and gave a second injection of serum directly into the wound.

For two weeks the child lay in the camp hospital having repeated hot Epsom salt baths for his injured foot. All seemed to be going well, when, on the fourteenth night, the child's neck glands became so swollen that he could not lie down. A nurse sat during the night holding him in her arms, the mosquito net from the child's bed thrown over them. The following morning, upon call, the Filipino doctor returned to see his young patient. The doctor applied ichthyol and a heavy bandage to the child's neck saying that there was a neck abscess which should be brought to a head.

During this period the internee doctor had prescribed nothing but had watched the case. When the Filipino had gone he removed the newly applied bandage, washed off the black salve and told the nurse that the child's swollen neck glands were the first sign of an allergic reaction to or of an overdose of tetanus antitoxin. Had there been a test injection? Had anyone checked on the exact amount of serum injected into the child's wound?

The child's neck glands swelled until he could not swallow. His head became so enlarged that his eyes were concealed in his puffed and distorted face. Hives came out over his body and in response to the nurse's urgent request a small amount of adrenalin was sold to the mother. The quantity was insufficient for proper treatment. The swelling continued until the interned doctor had to resort to puncturing the flesh to prevent rupture.

In the one room hospital there were at that time ten patients: two men, five women, two babies, and the injured child. There were no partitions for quiet or privacy. The moaning and sobbing of the sick child so annoyed one of the men patients that the boy was transferred to the children's quarters for the final month of treatment and recuperation.

In an effort to prevent the spread of communicable disease in the camp, internees underwent a series of injections by the Filipino doctor. Three injections of dysentery, typhoid, and cholera serum were gladly accepted despite the fact that the needles were of such dullness that several stabs were necessary to break the skin. There seemed to be no doubt but that blame for the spread of dysentery within the camp could be laid upon the flies which inhabited internee living quarters and shared internee food at mealtime. These flies could be traced to Japanese horses pastured in a field adjoining the camp and to the fishing village on the sea. But there was no protection from them; neither living quarters, kitchen-dining room, nor outdoor toilets were screened.

At the request of the internees a Filipino dentist was allowed in camp in July. He brought no electrical equipment and only a handful of instruments. There was no running water in the room where he worked; his patients sat in an ordinary chair. His main implements were pliers for extractions and a scalpel for hand-scraping decay before filling a tooth. The commandant advised the director that internees must pay for dental services in cash or in promissory notes, which resulted, needless to say, in much of the dental work being done on credit. A guard stood beside the dentist while he worked to prevent his talking with the patients.

There were two deaths in camp. A Mr. Williams from the Negros lumber mill had suffered a toe amputation shortly before internment and while in camp the infection spread over his foot. When the director pointed out to the commandant that there was danger to Mr. Williams' life unless the foot could be amputated and that there were neither anesthetics nor instruments in camp, the reply was, "If he dies, the Japanese will bury him."

The Japanese offer was accepted soon. When at the point of death, Mr. Williams was carried to the Japanese Army hospital in Bacolod and an amputation above the knee was performed; but surgery had been too long delayed. After a simple funeral service in the camp the body was carried away by the Japanese for burial.

The second internee death was also that of a man, a British employee of the lumber company. The rapid mental and physical deterioration which he suffered after internment first evidenced itself in lapse of memory and in loss of muscular coordination. With the passage of time he knew neither who nor where he was nor could he stand alone. Worse, he made attempts upon his own life and the lives of other internees with a razor. He was transferred to the Japanese Army hospital when cure was known to be impossible and death was near. He died in the hospital.

Within the camp a five foot wooden cross was made to go upon the Britisher's grave, the site of which had been selected by the Japanese. The cross was covered with hibiscus leaves and with purple clover from a small patch discovered in a corner of the grounds. Upon crude circular and oblong frames internees tied red hibiscus blossoms and leaves. When the body was brought briefly to camp before private Japanese burial a missionary read a short funeral sermon based on the theme "Death is a promotion."

One mother came into camp with two fresh goats to provide milk for her baby. Other parents were not so fortunate and the health of their children depended upon the mercy of the group. Following the decision to pool canned milk along with other foodstuffs a children's allowance was made from the milk. An apportionment was made for each child on the basis of age, the largest amounts going to infants.

When it became apparent that the canned milk would have to be stretched for an indefinite length of time fresh carabao milk was substituted. This was bought by the Swiss and delivered with other foodstuffs to the camp and, like them, was charged to the director's funds. The exhaustion of these moneys placed the purchase of milk upon an individual basis. Those without cash did without milk. Rice water was substituted for milk in the diet of most of the children.

On the camp menu appeared occasional special dishes for children: cassava pudding, eggs from the camp poultry, or tender cuts of camp livestock. These were not needed by the hospital and were in insufficient quantity for general use. However, efforts to abolish the preferential feeding of children were instigated by a middle aged woman, though there was at no time opposition to the special feeding of the sick. Objections to specialties for children, including milk, were based upon the claim that interned adults should not jeopardize their health in behalf of youth.

In September, a children's party further evidenced the unwillingness of a small minority group to permit preferential treatment of children. While making preparations for a camp party for all interned children the recreational leader in charge asked the director for refreshments of calamanci juice and rice flour cookies from the kitchen. Contrary to his personal feelings in the matter the director replied, "If the camp supplies special foods for a children's party there are adults who would complain." Contributions of money from parents made the purchase of a package of raspberry gelatin possible. This, in a pitcher of water, made a colorful, though tasteless, "pink-ade."

Resentment toward special treatment of children was complicated by the racial issue involved. There were more mestizo than white children in camp. Filipino, Indian, and Chinese blood was evidenced in children's skin colors ranging from dark brown through café au lait to creamy Caucasian. The original dissension from the plan to provide canned milk for all children was based upon the knowledge that pre-war food habits of dark skinned children varied from those of the whites. After the discontinuance of breast feeding the Filipino child's diet was similar to that of the Filipino adult: rice, fish, bananas, and native vegetables, with the American emphasis upon milk and eggs completely lacking.

However, any plan to classify the children and babies into those who needed milk and those who did not would have been extremely difficult. Should the division be made on the basis of food habits, racial heritage, or skin color? Some of the interned mestizos were among the wealthiest residents of the Islands and ate as did the Americans. The issue was further complicated by the fact that food contributions had been accepted from dark skinned adults as well as white.

There was no racial discrimination at any time in work assignments within the camp, or in the internee care given to the aged, the sick, and children.

6

Bacolod Camp Organization:
Recreation, Religion, and Communication

IN GENERAL, the Japanese were apathetic toward internee recreation. On only one occasion did the Japanese sponsor an entertainment program—the showing of an American movie the like of which internees had not seen for many years, if at all.

Internees sat upon the floor on the night of the movie and gazed at a sheet upon a classroom wall. First they saw Felix the Cat (predecessor of Mickey Mouse); then the Yale-Army football game of October, 1930; a Charlie Chaplin silent film; and a slow moving Laurel and Hardy episode of the period when women's dresses were waisted below the hips and befringed like old-fashioned lamp shades. The program was long and silent, and when men, women, and children pulled cramped legs from the floor there was not an individual who requested a repeat performance.

A former instructor in a Filipino boys' school exercised the greatest initiative in camp inspired recreation. He called for volunteers for baseball nines, horseshoe pitching teams, and a dramatics club. At his first baseball practice the erratic playing of British and Dutch internees who had never before participated in the game not only confused their coach but brought roars from the audience seated upon verandah steps, the grass, and atop toilet roofs. Baseball novices ran clockwise around the field, and omitted bases when they made a counter-clockwise circuit.

Horseshoe pitching was the favorite sport of the older

men. During siesta hours each afternoon the click of horse-shoes broke the camp stillness. The old men preferred to pitch rather than attempt to sleep.

The first of a dozen skits was held on July 29 when internee musical and dramatic talent entertained the camp at large. On this occasion men, women, and children gathered in the recreation room to listen to a Scotsman repeat humorous anecdotes in his native dialect, see four little girls (two dark and two white skinned) enact a doll's cradle song, and laugh with the Negro who demonstrated the types of snores heard nightly in his quarters.

Between the completion of the six o'clock roll call and the nine o'clock curfew, makeshift tables in the recreation room were in use for bridge and poker games while players sat uncomfortably upon school desks. Other internees read from the camp collection of about one hundred varied books, or studied Spanish in a conversation class.

Few holidays passed without attempted celebration. On July 4, decorations of red, white, and blue adorned the clothing or the bodies of men, women, and children. Women wore red hibiscus blossoms in their hair. As a special treat for the day the Swiss in Bacolod sent large blocks of ice, and while gay internees consumed it they were photographed by interested Japanese.

On August 31 Queen Wilhelmina's birthday was observed in the dining room. Yellow (in lieu of orange) leaves of the croton plant were tacked to the wall to spell out W-I-L-H-E-L-M-I-N-A and the date. Bowls of yellow leaves decorated desks where the Dutch priests sat, and a dessert of sliced yellow camotes concluded the meal. While the Dutch sang their national anthem in their native tongue other internees rose and gave three cheers for the queen.

November 26 was set aside as a day of Thanksgiving, regardless of the fact that President Roosevelt had decreed a change of date in America. The simultaneous appearance on this day of two rainbows across the morning sky was greeted by men and women as an omen of great magnitude.

Shouts of appreciation came from internees when they saw the Thanksgiving turkey which lay in state in the dining room at lunch time. From a large pumpkin, shaped surprisingly like the torso of a fowl, protruded legs of speckled bananas, while copper wire feet stuck high into the air. Curved slices of camotes provided wings. The turkey rested upon a platter of red rice, which, at a distance, might have been mistaken for the dressing it represented.

Months of hoarding and hand manufacture preceded Christmas as men and women drew upon their own resources for gift provisions. Not until the morning of December 25 was the full extent of preparations known. On this day, as all ages entered the dining room for breakfast, a strange and beautiful sight met their eyes. A lime tree which grew within the grounds had been cut and moved indoors. It glistened with flattened, polished tin can stars, and tin can animals surrounded its base. The tree was festooned with segments of red, blue, and brown wrapping paper.

Santa, in purple pajamas and rope fiber beard, appeared after a breakfast of rice cakes and coconut milk. From a slim bag upon his shoulders he withdrew balls crocheted of wrapping twine, small tin cups, wooden blocks, toy rakes and shovels—a hand-made gift for every child in camp. Bamboo knitting needles, wrapping string belts, coconut shell buttons and buckles, and animal bone rings were exchanged by adults later in the day as original evidences of old-fashioned good wishes.

Few toys had been brought into camp or could be manufactured there, and from the first, internee children amused themselves principally with stones and cans. In their games the children divided themselves into teams for a war-time version of cops and robbers. The cops were Americans; the robbers were Japanese. The skill of mestizo children in keeping a straw ball in the air by bouncing it against the inner ankle (an old Philippine game) was imitated by American children until they, too, became proficient in this oriental art.

Regular services were held by the various religious affiliations in the camp. The seven interned priests selected one of their number to conduct Sunday services and the others alternated at weekday mass. On Sunday evenings a Presbyterian missionary, assisted by a Baptist minister, conducted Protestant worship. Approximately one-third of the camp population participated in the religious program, though there were no externals to provide an atmosphere of sanctity in the bare recreation room. The church altar was the same table upon which internees played cards. A lectern (constructed from crude lumber found upon the grounds) placed upon this table served Protestants and Catholics alike.

In recognition of the depth of the faith of both missionaries and priests the camp was quiet at the hours of all religious services. Each major sect respected the privileges of the other. A new element in the religious life of camp was added with the arrival of three American Indians who followed a modified sun worship. The daily religious instruction which the Indian mother gave to her daughters so interested other internees that a few became regular attendants at the Indian religious observance.

Eighteen per cent of the camp population were religious professionals (Protestant missionaries, Catholic priests and nuns). No overt conversions into or withdrawals from any church occurred during the period of Bacolod internment, but the enforced contact between secular and clerical internees resulted in a new understanding (and a new evaluation on the part of the lay population) of church staffs in foreign fields.

Communications with the outside world were severely limited. Food and clothing gifts from uninterned friends, relatives, and servants trickled into camp. Notes were allowed to accompany these provided there was no mention of war or business affairs. Parcels and notes were handed to guards at the gate who turned them over to the commandant for inspection and censorship. Outgoing messages of thanks likewise went through the commandant's office where they were read and held until the addressee called at the gate.

No use of the mails was granted, and there was no correspondence except with individuals living close to the camp and in direct contact with it. Communications were limited, therefore, to a few foreign neutrals and to Filipinos in and near Bacolod who were willing to brave Japanese displeasure by coming to the camp. These came in decreasing numbers when Japanese pressure made camp visits both unpleasant and unsafe for outsiders.

Hiding in the mountains of Negros were small groups of Americans and British who had refused to give themselves up for internment. They were from the faculty of a missionary college and from one of the sugar centrals. Repeatedly the commandant urged internees to communicate with these friends, offering to send messages directly to the mountain hideouts upon internee direction. But the men and women in camp were honest in a denial of knowledge of the mountain retreats. It was suspected that the hiding aliens had joined Filipino guerrilla bands and lived a nomadic existence in the Negros wilderness.

No avenue of communication between the guerrillas and the internees was ever established. Guerrilla activities on Negros resulted in the burning of Japanese warehouses and soldiers' barracks within sight of internees but the guerrillas themselves made no attempt to enter the camp grounds.

During the nine months of the camp's existence no posted letters or packages were received by internees. British Red Cross parcels were delivered to Manila internees during this period, but these failed to find their way to Negros "enemy aliens."

Efforts to discover from the Japanese the location and the personnel of other civilian and military camps were futile, for no communication between camps was permitted. The husbands of two interned women were supposedly in other camps but the commandant refused to confirm or deny the rumor. In a futile effort to contact the spouses from whom they were separated the two wives gave un-addressed notes to the commandant asking him to carry out their delivery, but later evidence disclosed that the notes were destroyed. When the food situation became critical, the director handed the commandant a letter to the International Red Cross in Manila asking for aid. Since no reply was received there was little reason to believe this letter left the commandant's office.

Occasional visitors were permitted to talk with men and women in the presence of a Japanese interpreter. Visitors, like note senders, were forbidden to mention the war or business conditions in the Islands. Filipino relatives of American men most frequently entered on passes, though other Filipinos and neutrals came to the gate with small gifts of eggs, carabao milk, vegetables, and fruit. During the first month visitors were allowed two mornings each week but as time passed fewer visitors were allowed and the duration of the visits was shortened. Sometimes camp visitors were limited to five minutes of conversation.

On at least one occasion the commandant utilized a visitor's pass to secure information valuable to the Japanese. A Filipino from the mountains where twenty-two internees had stored personal possessions had been refused camp entrance for several months when suddenly his application for a pass was granted. He was given permission to talk with all internees who had left goods stored with him. In the presence of the commandant he answered questions concerning the looting of these supplies by hungry Filipinos and the quantities which remained. He also told of the whereabouts of other Filipinos who had been left as caretakers. From these talks the commandant culled two useful bits of information: the location of supplies in which the Japanese were interested and the residence of a Filipino nurse whom they sought for conscription work in a Japanese military hospital.

There were no attempts to escape from the camp, for internee homes had been looted, burned, or occupied by the

Japanese, and lack of transportation discouraged any effort to reach the seclusion of the mountains to the north and east of Bacolod. Toward the sea, to the west, Bacolod's piers were scenes of Japanese activity, and Panay Island, the nearest land refuge, had suffered prior occupation and greater destruction than Negros. To the south lay Bacolod, Japanese Army headquarters. Skin color and stature of foreigners made them conspicuous among natives with whom they might attempt to hide, and interned Filipinos felt such fear of the Japanese Army that they believed themselves to be as secure within the camp as without.

The number of interned women, children, and old people was insurance against organized mass escape or rebellion. Women made up one-third of the camp population and children accounted for another fifth. The smallness of the group also militated against organized resistance, for soldiers quartered within sight of the camp generally outnumbered the prisoners.

In an effort to protect the camp from group reprisals for individual outbursts of hostility, men and women were urged by the director to communicate with the commandant only through him. This request was the result of the following incident:

At morning roll call a few days after the opening of camp the commandant asked for an explanation of internee absences. The director replied that absentees were too sick to leave their quarters. The interned doctor interrupted to add that the illnesses were directly traceable to the refusal of the Japanese to allow him to bring medical supplies from his hospital. The commandant's face flushed at this public accusation and he angrily threatened action against the group if similar outbursts occurred again.

Knowing little about the outside world, interned men and women pieced together bits of fact with fancy to create war rumors. Hong Kong was "officially" retaken from the Japanese four times during 1942, though the source of such information was seldom disclosed by the informant.

As rumored forces closed in upon the Islands in 1943 internees discussed at great length which might be expected first: the Australians from their homeland, the Dutch from the Indies, the British from Malaya, or the Americans from across the Pacific. Though Americans expressed a preference for release by troops of their own nationality, they nevertheless listened eagerly to rumors of advances of others in their behalf. Optimistic expectancy was punctured somewhat when an internee tacked upon the wall a quotation from a library book: "The prisoner, the solitary, thinking day and night of his own sad fate, is always inclined to believe that those who live in the free and active world must be thinking as much about him as he thinks about himself. Of course, it is not so."[1]

Rumors occasionally proved true. A camp story that the Swiss of the Islands had been offered free passage to Chile by the Japanese was later verified by the Bacolod neutrals. However, none of the latter wished to leave an uncertain known situation for an equally uncertain new one.

Sometimes rumors related to the camp itself. One day a Filipino coconut vendor had an opportunity of whispering to an internee that twenty-three American Army officers who had been imprisoned in a small schoolhouse in the center of Bacolod had been transferred to Manila. Civilian

[1] Stefan Zweig, *Mary Queen of Scotland and the Isles* (New York: Viking Press, 1935), p. 285.

internees had never seen the other prisoners but had heard that they were confined in Bacolod. "Now that these men have been transferred," the peddler added, "it is told among the Japanese that your camp is to be discontinued also." This news was received with mixed feelings of fright, joy, and relief. Those who were most anxious to believe what the Filipino said were, however, the first to discount his report as just another rumor.

A limitless source of rumor as well as of propaganda was the Japanese commandant's office. On the first of several occasions for the public dissemination of "news" the commandant invited internees to his office for a July evening broadcast. His office was filled immediately the invitation was issued; others crowded the door. A clear radio announcement came in English: "Britain is on the verge of complete collapse. The United States has decided not to send aid to the Far East. Japanese forces are approaching the American shores." After the program a woman asked the commandant, "Have the Japanese landed on the United States mainland?" "Not yet," he replied, "but very soon it will be the United States of Japan. Then you can go home for the war will be over."

As further fuel for speculation the commandant offered to internees a dateless magazine, "Nippon Philippines," published in Tokyo in English, Tagalog (the most widely spoken Philippine dialect), and in Malay. The magazine was profusely illustrated with photographs of Japanese plane production and of capital ships of the Japanese Navy. There were pictures of the surrender of Corregidor and of the booty captured at Syonan (Singapore) and at Hong Kong. The following war statistics were credited to Japan:

War planes shot down and destroyed				3,910
Tanks destroyed or captured				1,440
Artillery " " "				3,763
Machine guns " " "				11,548
Rifles " " "				216,714
Motor trucks " " "				31,584
Railway cars " " "				12,220
Shipping seized				220,000 tons
Shipping sunk or damaged				1,419,000 tons
War prisoners				342,000

The leading article of the magazine had nothing to do with the war, however. It was captioned "Long Live Nippon's Silk" and featured Nipponese bathing beauties in abbreviated beach costumes of silk. There was a comic section with subtitles in three languages, the first cartoon being a full page caricature of MacArthur. Above the words "Sacked in Australia" MacArthur was shown hiding in the pouch of a huge kangaroo, only his arm sticking out to receive a sealed envelope from a United States soldier. Hanging on MacArthur's arm was a lady's undergarment, and his military boots and a lady's high heeled slipper rested beside the concealing kangaroo. In small letters were the words, "MacArthur, the newly appointed commander-in-chief of the kangaroo battalion, receiving orders from President Roosevelt."

Another cartoon showed four American soldiers marching forward, eyes fixed upon crosses which they held before them in their hands. The soldiers were captioned "Onward Christian Soldiers." The same four soldiers were pictured returning, bandages covering their disfigured bodies, un-

der the words "Backward Red Cross Soldiers." The clever-
est of the cartoons showed a distracted queen peering
through a lorgnette at a globe upon a pedestal. In one
hand she held a bunch of poppies. Said the queen, "We
urgently need a new continent or island now that our East
Indies have been lost."

Rumors in the Bacolod camp developed as a result of
curtailed communication with the outside world. Both
wishful thinking and anxieties gave direction to these rumors. The general aspects of war-time rumors are discussed more fully in Chapter 10.

The Japanese

THE first Bacolod commandant was a lieutenant in the regular Japanese Army who had entered the Islands from Japan with invading forces. He told internees that his ability to speak and understand English was the determining factor in his selection for the camp position.

Lieutenant Nagasi was twenty-nine years old and had had five years of military training prior to the outbreak of war. In an officer training school he had chosen English when faced with the compulsion of learning German, English, or Italian. He spoke English well and used a wide vocabulary with little accent. He was tall, for a Japanese, and immaculate in his officer's uniform.

Lieutenant Nagasi's friendliness and sometimes generosity towards internees seemed to be the result of changing motivation. He brought a pony into the camp for the children to ride because, he said, he had small brothers and sisters in Japan. He sat upon the internees' verandah and chatted when nostalgia for Japan overtook him. On one such occasion he pulled from his pocket a woman's gold wrist watch which he had secured in Bacolod for his fiancée in Japan, and he passed it around for internee praise.

Lieutenant Nagasi's periods of comradeship with the men and women under his supervision were often followed by periods of avoidance, during which he appeared to be disdainful of associating with his prisoners. Nagasi's vacillating moods caused internees to become suspicious of his approaches toward intimacy.

During one of his periods of intercourse with internees

Nagasi explained interesting customs of the Japanese Army. Men in the camp had noticed the guards as they lined themselves each dawn for a rising sun ceremony. The soldiers began a daily chant in the semi-darkness as they faced the camp. When the first rays of the sun appeared they turned in unison and faced the east and the chant was completed with eyes focused upon the sun itself.

Lieutenant Nagasi was asked the meaning of the rising sun salute. He explained that when a Japanese soldier is stationed in the homeland he faces east to greet the rising sun; if the soldier is stationed outside his homeland he faces Japan. Since the Philippine Islands had become a part of the Japanese Empire the soldiers faced the rising sun itself. The chanted salutation contained the following five pledges: 1. To dedicate life to the Emperor; 2. To be courteous; 3. To maintain healthy bodies, to be good fighters; 4. To be truthful; 5. To be frugal.[1]

Lieutenant Nagasi, with his military bearing, glistening boots, and shining saber was the cynosure of the children's attention. A movie camera which hung from a leather shoulder strap further increased his stature in the eyes of interned youth. Nagasi was an enthusiastic amateur photographer, the favorite subject for his pictures being himself. While an instructed guard turned film Nagasi posed with white children on his shoulders, holding his hands, bowing and smiling toward him. He preferred blonde children for these photographs, and he found all the children willing and eager cooperators. Adults also smiled for the lieutenant's pictures with the hope that their agreeableness

---

[1] The above pledge is a condensation of the Imperial Rescript to Soldiers and Sailors, granted the fourth day of the first month of the fifteenth year of Meiji (1882).

might in some manner result in the pictures' reaching the eyes of understanding families and friends outside the occupation zone.

Efforts to secure food for the camp brought a request from Nagasi for patience. Though he insisted that internee well being was his sole concern, it soon became evident that he had interests outside camp. He was seldom in his office or on the grounds, and when he returned after long absences he was irritated by requests.

Prohibited from direct contact with army headquarters and limited to communication with them through Nagasi, internees were stalemated. It was with a sense of relief, therefore, that the camp learned that the ambivalent Nagasi was leaving. When the lieutenant informed the camp that a Japanese civilian was taking his place, he left his Japan address with internees and asked for correspondence after the war.

The new commandant was a carpenter, Yasamari, for twenty-two years a laborer on a Negros sugar central. He had risen from workshop to administrator's polished desk by the chances of war. Mari, as he was known locally, appeared at camp with a smug smile of self-satisfaction upon his face for Yasamari's former employer was one of his prisoners. To him Mari assigned the job of mopping his office each morning. Mari was fed in the camp (with food internees bought) and slept on a mat put down in his office each night. It was felt by internees that Japanese military authorities placed Mari in charge of the camp to humiliate them, for he had no real power and had to refer to Japanese headquarters in Bacolod all requests and complaints made to him.

Yasamari's carelessness of his person was revolting. His clothing was dirty; his body was dirty, and he walked around in bare feet caked with mud. He dressed fairly well the first few days he was in office but soon reverted to his pre-war laborer's habits. When Mari wore a shirt he left it open from neck to waist, exposing his bare chest and his navel, for his trousers hung so low they seemed in constant danger of falling. As he became more slovenly and careless about himself, he became more insistent that internees show him the respect he thought his due. He demanded not only bowing, but deep bowing, and made threats for noncompliance.

Internees who entered the office of the commandant bowed at the door, bowed again at his desk before addressing him, and bowed upon departure from the room. At roll call internees bowed in unison before their names were checked. At the conclusion of roll call they bowed. They bowed before passing guards.

Toddlers had difficulty in making bowing distinctions. If they were able to stand they were required to bow. Children became so well indoctrinated with the bowing principle that some of them, upon rising from bed in the morning, bowed solemnly to mothers who had slept beside them.

As a result of the bowing regulation, the approach of a guard or the commandant became a signal for disappearance. Sleeping quarters and the out-buildings swallowed men, women, and children until the Japanese had passed. In spite of this consistent emphasis upon the bowing salutation there seemed to be no uniform Japanese response. Sometimes the guards or the commandant bowed in return. More humiliating were those compulsory body bendings which were deliberately ignored.

Yasamari interpreted his privilege of opening internee gifts for inspection to include the sampling of foodstuffs. On more than one occasion he took as his toll more than remained for the intended recipient.

Lieutenant Nagasi commanded the respect of the guards who patrolled the grounds and the area outside the fence. These soldiers worked in shifts and reported at each change to Nagasi as a superior army officer. Yasamari, on the other hand, had no military background and had had no contact with Japan or the Japanese people for many years. He had spent his adult life in the Philippines, had married a Filipino, and sired children who called themselves Filipinos. His knowledge of the Japanese language and his experiences on Negros since the outbreak of war were his sole ties with the invaders.

In December, 1941, in the hysteria which followed the first Japanese attack upon the Islands, Filipino constabulary had immediately rounded up resident Japanese nationals. Among those taken into custody on Negros was Yasamari. He had been confined in the Bacolod North Elementary School with others born in Japan or of Japanese ancestry. The fence around the school grounds had been electrified and barbed wire had been nailed across Yasamari's windows. His protests that he was innocent of connivance with the invading Japanese were undoubtedly true, for his American employer certified that there had been no evidence of contact between Mari and his homeland for many years. However, Yasamari's release from internment was not accomplished by the Americans and Filipinos with whom he had long been associated, but by the military might of the Japanese. Yasamari was embittered and vindictive toward both Americans and Filipinos who, he felt, had betrayed him. He welcomed the opportunity of becoming commandant.

But Yasamari was not equipped by training or personality to hold the respect of the Japanese guards under his command. From the first there was conflict between them. The acceptance of packages for internees by the guards at the gate brought Mari rushing from his office. He reprimanded the guards and snatched parcels from their hands. Visitors entering the gate on passes approved by the guards were ordered out again by Mari. Yet friends of Mari, without credentials, were allowed to enter over protests of the guards. Visitors' passes were issued only by army headquarters in Bacolod.

As the months passed Mari directed his abusive energies toward the guards rather than internees, creating an intra-Japanese conflict which lessened, rather than increased, opportunity for amelioration of the internee lot. When the guards carried their fight to military headquarters Mari was called for an explanation, but no military investigation of the camp resulted. Mari, as commandant, still represented internees to the military from whom they sought food. He was sole spokesman in their behalf. Mari's break with the military command caused the expectation of aid from that source to diminish, and internees concentrated less upon the Japanese and more upon their own efforts toward self-sufficiency.

Since the guards were responsible to the commandant, their insubordination was one of the chief characteristics of Mari's tenure. Throughout Mari's administration the guards were out of hand and complaints about them from internees were futile. They amused themselves by sitting in their second-story windows across the road from the camp with field glasses focused into internee bedroom interiors. Since the sparse camp furnishings brought by internees did not include shades or curtains, and the rooms were too hot to close the solid windows each time a modest internee wished to dress, the only recourse for privacy was to duck beneath the window sill. The guards also peeked into toilets, showers, and bedroom windows as they walked about the grounds.

These trespasses upon personal privacy were no more vexing than were other activities of the guards. On one occasion, while internees watched through the fence, an American flag was torn and tied to posts to mark off a cotton field near camp where Filipino recruits in the Japanese Army were practicing war maneuvers. The destruction of the flag was a Japanese effort to add zest to the field activity of Filipinos who had deserted the American cause as well as to annoy internee spectators.

Further evidences of the increasing assertiveness of the guards were the drinking celebrations in military quarters adjacent to the camp. The first was a despedida (farewell party) for soldiers preparing to go to the front. Internees had watched soldiers packing uniforms and other belongings during the day and had seen bedding carried to boats at the pier. At nightfall the party got under way. Empty beer and saki bottles which were tossed through the guards' windows fell on the camp grounds. The panes of a closed window were crashed as the bottles came through. The affair ended in a free-for-all when one soldier hit another over the head with a rifle. Internees watching from the verandah scuttled to their rooms, fearing stray shots. At dawn the next morning the now somewhat sobered soldiers sang as they rode to waiting transports.

During another beer and saki celebration drunken guards entered the grounds. It was not yet nine o'clock and internees were again sitting and standing on the verandahs. A woman was slapped across the face, another upon her back before a sober guard ordered the drunken ones away. In the history of the camp this incident was the only one of physical abuse by the Japanese. Neglect and less obvious means of torture than bodily mishandling characterized Bacolod captor-internee relations.

The misfortunes of individual men and women had repercussions throughout the camp. The separation by the Japanese of a young mother from her husband and three small children and the tragedy which befell them is a case in point. The mother, twenty-six years old, was interned but her children—aged six, four, and three—were compelled to remain outside camp with their neutral father. The children were seldom allowed passes to visit camp, but each afternoon at five o'clock they walked, accompanied by their father or a Filipino amah, beside the camp fence. There was no waving, no signaling, no sign of recognition between the children and their mother for the guards watched them closely. In rainy weather as well as in sunshine the two little boys and their sister came out for their mother to have her silent look at them, after which they turned and went back solemnly to their home.

The father had served in the USAFFE but had not been held by the Japanese because of his Spanish-Philippine citizenship. Reportedly a Filipino who had accused the former USAFFE member of locating, for the Japanese, United States Army supplies entered the soldier's home on an early evening and shot him as he sat reading, holding his four year old son in his arms. The child's head was blown to pieces by the explosion, the shell passing through the body of the father. Servants fled from the house, leaving the two surviving children, a boy of six and a girl of three, eye witnesses to the murder, to spend the night alone with the bleeding corpses.

The Japanese, to whom the affair was reported, buried the bodies and took the remaining children to relatives in a nearby town. It was then that the Japanese sent a representative to tell the mother what had taken place. The mother begged the Japanese to let her go to her son and daughter—to be with them in privacy for a few days to recover from the shock. "Once a person is placed in concentration camp confinement," the Japanese explained, "she cannot be permitted out again."

The mother became hysterical. Only upon the urgent insistence of the internee doctor and the director did the Japanese bring the boy and girl to camp.

"Aren't you glad to see me?" asked the boy of six when the stolid expression on his mother's face failed to change. "If you are glad, then you will smile."

"Then I shall smile for you," replied the mother, and the observing doctor and internees saw the first evidence of her return to normalcy after shock.

The wire fence afforded a clear view of Japanese activities beyond the confines of the camp. Some of these were actions of brutality; others were concerned with Japanese looting and Japanese agricultural policy. These outside observations were a strong factor in raising or depressing hopes within.

The camp was so situated that glimpses of the sea appeared through a coconut grove. The palms sheltered a tiny fishing village of nipa huts beyond which the Bacolod pier extended into the shallow water. Here Japanese boats loaded and discharged their cargoes. Into Bacolod from the ships came fully equipped soldiers; out of Bacolod to the pier went truck loads of rice and sugar, second-hand bicycles and typewriters. Filled alcohol drums indicated at least one Island sugar mill distillery in operation. Trucks on the pier road passed so close to the camp that the names of their pre-war owners were clearly discernible upon them. The Japanese made no effort to erase these.

Internees watched an oil storage tank near the pier tediously dismantled and loaded on waiting boats. Trucks of scrap iron from the north and from the south converged to fill waiting holds. The methodical, unhasty looting procedure of the Japanese caused internees as great discouragement as any phase of the occupation policy. The deliberateness and completeness of the destruction was further illustrated by the razing of a red roofed bungalow a few hundred yards from the camp fence. Flowering bougainvillea was torn from arched trellises. Metal was stripped from roof and gutters. Beams, walls, window frames, doors were transported away. Removal of the flooring was followed by the careful collection from the ground of nails which had dropped during the razing process.

The removal of the bungalow by the Japanese brought into clearer camp view the Japanese crematorium which lay beyond. This crematorium—a long concrete vat, open at the top—was the former garbage disposal incinerator for the city of Bacolod. It was near the highway, in a field, protected from the rain by a sideless shelter. The first noted Japanese action at the incinerator was the clearing away of unconsumed rubbish and the repairing of the gullied road from the highway. Later, it was with a sense of revulsion that internees realized the Japanese plan to utilize the vat for the cremation of their dead.

A hearse and military escort accompanied the first bodies for cremation, though subsequent bodies came to the pyre attended only by crematorium workers. Wood was used in the long, slow, cremation process, and when the wind was from the north the odor of burning flesh so permeated the camp that men and women sought work on the south grounds as a slight escape. Smoke from the crematorium led internees in north quarters to close windows despite the tropical heat. Physically, internees suffered no harm from the location of the crematorium; psychologically, the forced sensory participation in a repelling activity caused keen distress.

An important phase of the Island occupation policy dealt with the re-education of Filipinos. This policy was evidenced in the posters appealing to Filipinos to align themselves with the Japanese against Americans—to form an oriental racial union to fight a common white oppressor. Internees were advised by the Japanese that supplies could not be brought to camp with the assistance of Filipino servants, for the day of servanthood for Filipinos had ended. At the same time Filipinos were informed that they were "free." The bewilderment of Filipinos at such a proclamation was matched by that of the Americans. Two illustrations of Negros Japanese-Filipino relations witnessed by internees will indicate the general reaction of Filipinos:

In June, 1942, at the hacienda where a sugar central staff and friends spent the night en route from the mountains to the camp, the Filipino hacendero showed the camp-bound foreigners several large native grass baskets. These were tightly packed and marked with the names of the members of his Filipino household. "There is one package for each person to carry in his arms in case we flee on a moment's notice. We expect any day to make a quick get-a-way to the mountains. The Japanese tell us not to be afraid, but we fear for our lives. The nervous strain of living like this is tremendous. You are wise to give yourselves up to the Japanese. We are Filipinos, but we are not safe."

The following incident, which occurred in January, 1943, illustrates the soundness of the Filipino's fears: A Filipino, returning at dusk to the seacoast village near camp was accosted by one of the guards at the gate. The Filipino was walking toward camp on the roadway from the highway. He was carrying a bunch of coconuts on one end of a bamboo pole, balanced by a bundle of dirty clothes upon the other. Evidently he did not understand the words called to him in Japanese, for he continued walking. A shot from the guard's gun stopped him in his tracks and startled all internees. The guard, accompanied by other soldiers, ran toward the Filipino. The guard slapped his face first with his palm and then with the back of his hand. The offending Filipino was taken to the guards' house. Here he was slapped many times before being carried off, his hands tied behind him, in the direction of Bacolod. The final scene of this incident was the Japanese guards eating the coconuts the Filipino had left behind.

Yasamari came out of his office at the sound of the shot and, noting interest in the affair, offered the information that the Japanese had that day placed a sign on the road traversed by the Filipino advising that the roadway was no longer a public thoroughfare. An internee asked Mari, "Do the guards not know that the Filipinos from the village to which he was returning are illiterate?" Yasamari shrugged his shoulders without further comment.

Truck loads of Filipino laborers, guarded by armed Japanese, passed camp to work in nearby sugar cane fields. They plowed the cane under and replanted the soil in cotton in an agricultural experiment which men and women inside the fence watched as closely as did the Japanese outside. Filipino laborers came daily to remove the smallest sign of competing vegetation or insect pests. Japanese made weekly inspection tours, arriving at the fields in polished automobiles, the officers white gloved.

For many years Americans had tried without satisfactory results to produce a commercial cotton crop in the Islands. The Japanese, long experienced in agriculture, had undertaken to plant, scientifically, Chinese varieties as well as American cotton. In March, when the fields were abloom, the Bacolod camp was closed, and it was not until their release from Santo Tomas two years later that results of the Negros experiment were made known to the internees. Filipinos reported that the Japanese cotton produced many blossoms, few bolls, and almost no fiber. Philippine soil and climate, well suited to the growth of cane, had again refused the successful production of badly needed raw material for clothing.

Several Japanese holiday celebrations were observed through the fence. On the eighth day of the eighth month —the double eighth—a cavalry parade passed before the grounds. Mounted soldiers ignored internees but the horses they rode were identified as coming from internee stables. Another parade and extra flags upon the guards' houses celebrated the establishment of the Philippine puppet government. On this occasion an outdoor loudspeaker installed so the guards could hear a Manila broadcast provided internees also with a day of entertainment.

On December 8, Filipinos celebrated the first anniversary of the outbreak of war. The gaiety began the night of December 7 when large Japanese barracks which had been erected near the pier went up in flames. Bacolod Filipinos were literally burning the Japanese out. While men, women, and children gathered at back windows to watch the bright conflagration, four terrific explosions from the front rocked internee quarters. The nearness of the activities startled the camp. Internees quickly extinguished lights and rushed out to see what was going on.

A two-story brick house on a knoll in one of the cotton fields was in flames. This house, in which Japanese officers had been living, had been dynamited. In the distance other fires lighted the horizon, and the Bacolod sky once more took on the rosy night glow as of cane fields being burned over after the sugar crop had been harvested, but the cane fields had long since been abandoned or plowed under. As far as the eye could see Filipino guerrillas were destroying their own property which had been appropriated by the Japanese.

The air was heavy with smoke all day of the eighth, and before dusk other fires, obviously of incendiary origin, broke out. Electricians had come to camp early in the morning to string wires outside the walls of the quarters building and to attach large bulbs at building corners and exits. Evidently the Japanese feared what internees half expected —that the celebrating Filipinos might attempt to enter camp, for there was evidence that guerrillas were becoming stronger and bolder as time went on. Not long before, when the Japanese had attempted to set in motion the alcohol distillery at a north Negros sugar central, their guards stationed at the central were attacked by a band of armed guerrillas. There were deaths on both sides, but the distillery equipment was destroyed by the guerrillas before they returned to their hideout in a wilderness which the Japanese did not dare to penetrate.

As a Japanese personality, Colonel Ota, in command of the Imperial Japanese Army on Negros, was a camp favorite. His appearance and his unintentional humor provided material for limitless comment. It was he, who, on his first visit to camp, asked to see women internees alone. Somewhat surprised at this request the women gathered in the recreation room and were seated on low school benches or standing against the wall when the colonel arrived. He was pigmy small. He seemed to be nothing but polished boots, a brightly shining saber, and a black, flowing mustache. The concealed lips opened, however, and the colonel repeated, in the memorized song of a school boy: "Life is like an ocean wave. Sometimes we are on the crest of the wave; sometimes we are in the hollow. When we are down we must keep our spirits high by work and by being happy. You have been far better treated here than have Japanese civilians in the United States. I hope that the war will end soon and that I may see some of you pleasantly in your own homes in America and England.

"Remember the spirit of Bushido [the colonel patted his chest heartily in the area of his heart]. Keep your spirits up and your courage and good will high. Take good care of your health. I have brought a remembrance with me [cigarettes] and from the bottom of my heart [more beating loudly upon his chest], I bid you now good-by."

There was applause from the women. The colonel reached deep into his trouser and military coat pockets and pulled out packages of "Cherry Brand" Japanese cigarettes which he passed around to his audience. Even the non-smokers—including the nuns—took cigarettes for the not-so-fortunate men. As women filed from the room each bowed and then shook the extended hand of the colonel. As he stood by the door, the upright position of the formerly droopy mustache indicated a smile.

Colonel Ota left Negros shortly after his speech. His successor was less generous (he brought no cigarettes) and less colorful. He was equally an enigma, however. After consistently refusing to act upon internee requests for food, the new colonel arranged for delivery of produce and cash while making preparations to discontinue the camp. Despite these last-minute feeding arrangements of the colonel, internees were puzzled by his announcement that they were to be "charged" for electricity and water used during the internment.

The bill which the new colonel submitted to internees included the use of the camp water supply by Filipino laborers who, under Japanese supervision, had sprayed cotton fields with a solution prepared in tanks near the camp fence. Water for the spray had at first been brought in buckets from a nearby spring. Then, a Japanese guard discovered that a bamboo trough could be attached to a faucet within the camp grounds and pulled through the fence. Once the camp faucet was turned on it ran all day—not only for the spraying solution but for open air baths for workers as well. This water, diverted outside the camp, was charged against internees by the Japanese.

The Japanese with whom internees had come in contact in the internee-guardian relationship remained inscrutable. Internees knew little more about the Japanese after months of internment than before the war. Yet hardly had the Japanese landed their conquering forces in the Philippines before a strong clue to one phase of their hidden nature became evident. The appearance in the Bacolod market of Kamel, Lucky Stroke, Cesterfild, and Pidmon cigarettes, and of de Lux and Lifeboat soap (in wrappings startlingly familiar in design and color) hinted at a peculiar talent vested in the invader. A similar duplicating of foreign goods had been noticeable before the war. What amazed internees was that the Japanese, while belittling their American enemies, were attempting at the same time to deceive their own people and the Filipinos into thinking they were getting superior American products.

8

Development of Artifacts
in the Bacolod Camp

"THE bulk of all cultures consists of what are, from the practical point of view, embroideries upon the fabric of existence."[1] The overt expressions of culture are referred to as culture traits, which may be divided into (a) individual actions and (b) artifacts or objects.[2] The customary "embroideries upon the fabric of existence" were torn to cultural tatters within the Bacolod camp. Substitutional embroideries resulted in a patchwork of traits peculiar to the internment situation.

Gillin[3] notes that society may be studied at three levels: (1) the pattern level (cultural patterns which serve as plans or specifications for social activities as a whole), (2) the activity level, and (3) the materialistic level. This chapter deals primarily with the third approach to the Bacolod camp culture. It is an examination of the material products and equipment which were developed within the camp. When the absence of customary products (soap, for instance) led to new activities (in this case, new laundry methods) these activities will be examined also.

The Bacolod internment camp culture became a mosaic of original traits interspersed among already established oriental and occidental artifacts and activities. Camp traits were adopted as the result of one of the following processes:

[1] Ralph Linton, *The Study of Man* (New York: Appleton-Century, 1936), p. 301.
[2] *Op. cit.*, p. 397.
[3] John Gillin, "Custom and Range of Human Response," *Character and Personality*, XIII (1944), 101-134.

FOR TOILET AND BATH

LIFEBOAT

LIFEBOAT

LIFEBOAT
HEALTH SOAP

FOR TOILET AND BATH

Germs of many common diseases may
be spread by hands. LIFEBOAT'S rich
soothing lather, with its exclusive
ingredient, helps remove germs as well as
dirt. Wash hands always with LIFEBOAT
HEALTH SOAP, especially before meals.

LIFEBOAT IS MADE IN P. I.

BY KIREN SOAP FACTORY

(1) trial and error technique, (2) symbolic experimentation (through discussion rather than direct experimentation), or (3) selection of appropriate idiosyncratic habits as group customs.

The first method, trial and error, was wasteful of time, human strength, and material. This was demonstrated by the unsuccessful efforts with tin cans, bottles, and misshapen coconuts before satisfactory drinking and eating utensils were evolved. Repeated attempts to use untanned leather were fruitless. Though the conservation of time (in terms of minutes, hours, days) was not a significant factor in camp life, the conservation of limited human energy was of the utmost importance. In the abuse of the latter and in the waste of scarce basic materials was the trial and error method especially unsatisfactory.

Group discussion of methods and goals prior to actual experimentation with materials made short-cuts in the trial and error method. Thus the representational contributions of several internees regarding wet and dry season tropical agriculture, camp soil analysis, and the nutritive value of plants led to the selection of certain methods of gardening and of indigenous species before the actual undertaking of a camp garden program. Thus were eliminated many pitfalls to crop success. Also in the hand carving of bakias,[4] the advantages and disadvantages of the curved and flat sole were weighed by discussion before construction was actually begun. The discarding of the curved bottom for camp use was proved (by later personal experimentation with this type of bakia) to have been wise.

The third method, of incorporating idiosyncratic habits into the camp mosaic, was the most simplified way of attain-

---

[4] Native footwear; a wooden sole with a single toe strap.

ing satisfactory cultural ends. Group adoption of individually used substitute materials for toothpaste and tobacco illustrate this method. Minor idiosyncratic habits of speech and dress also had camp-wide imitation. For instance, the "hyah" of a British subject replaced the American "here" as an answer to daily roll call. This gave evidence of the general prestige of the British within the camp. The prewar practice of dress of one internee family—the use of a drawstring instead of elastic in men's, women's, and children's underpants—also became a part of the camp culture.

Substitutional artifacts and methods of work became immediately necessary. An early checkup of supplies brought into the Bacolod camp indicated insufficient eating and cooking utensils to satisfy daily needs. Chinaware, glasses, knives, forks, spoons, pots, and pans were in the possession, in limited supply, of individual internees, and a request from the director that these be turned over to the camp kitchen and dining room met with a generous response. The initial shortage of such materials was, however, soon aggravated by breakage impossible of replacement. It became evident that large numbers of eating and drinking vessels would have to be developed from materials within the camp.

A mug or a cup was essential to camp life. Hot coffee, though weak and made from a poor quality of native bean, was the mainstay of the adult. Men and women also discovered that repeated drinking of hot water mitigated the effects of a starchy diet. Children constantly required cups or mugs for carabao milk or broth received through the camp kitchen.

The use in the kitchen of a rotary can opener left emptied

tins with a smoothly rolled edge. Around these cans stiff wire was encircled near top and bottom. Twisted wire was then elongated into a firm handle to provide a thoroughly satisfactory and unbreakable drinking necessity. Soon, however, it was noticed that exposure to hot liquids and to atmospheric moisture caused insides of the tins to rust. Experiments with "gold lined" tins, used in the preservation of acid fruit and vegetable products, showed these to have more corrosion resistance. Pliers, wire, and a can were all that was necessary to provide each individual with his own gold lined cup.

With the passage of months gold lined cans rusted and the kitchen supply of tins was exhausted. Internees looked longingly at empty beer and whisky bottles which had accumulated from Japanese use and had been left upon the camp garbage dump. The smooth removal of the bottle necks would produce a rust proof mug. But no one knew how to sever the necks smoothly and evenly at the desired spot.

A former Boy Scout came forward to suggest that a string be saturated in oil and tied around each bottle at the desired place of partition. When the string was lighted the bottle broke at the point of contact. The sharp edge which remained was smoothed with stones, but it was difficult to rub it sufficiently to prevent the edge from cutting the lips.

In the meantime another internee had been working upon a more satisfactory method of de-necking the bottles and had developed a device for this purpose. He had twisted wire into a hinged circle the approximate size of the bottles to be cut. Two long wire handles permitted opening or closing of the circular form. This simple mechanism he heated in an open fire, placed around the bottle and held in position while the bottle was dipped into cold water. However, difficulties in hinging the wire and burns which resulted to internees led to the abandonment of this method.

A third procedure proved the most effective for removing bottle necks. Bottles were filled with water to the desired level of cleavage and a few drops of oil or melted fat were poured into the bottle. A lighted splinter dropped inside caused a clean break. Wire bands and handles from the cans were adjusted to fit the glass mugs.

Next, coconut-shell bowls were manufactured for the dining room. Filipinos who worked in nearby groves sold nuts to internees for making coconut milk (oil and juice squeezed from grated coconut meat) for use in the kitchen in the preparation of meals. Discarded coconut shells had served as kitchen fuel. The increasing need for plates and bowls, however, led to their utilization for eating utensils.

Coconuts were opened in such a manner that the spherical surface containing the eyes—the weakest part of the shell—was small. The remainder made a deep, concave vessel. To facilitate cleaning the bowls the rough outer fiber was rubbed smooth and both outer and inner surfaces were polished until they shone. The failure of early bowls to maintain a steady balance when filled with liquid led to the later selection from Filipino merchants of flat-ended coconuts with favorable "bowl-setting" qualities. Coconut shells also provided the raw material for dining room and kitchen spoons. These were made by attaching, with wire, stick handles to rounded pieces of smooth shell.

Another internee project was shoe repair and manufacture. The hides of slaughtered animals were dried in the sun preliminary to their anticipated use for shoe repairs.

The first few efforts with untanned leather made its useless-
ness apparent, however, for with every attempt to sew or
nail the skins they cracked and split.

The absence of shoes became acute, for the necessary
out-of-door camp activities in rain and heat were destruc-
tive to leather. Mothers became frightened lest their children who were forced to go barefooted get tropical parasites
into their bodies from the contaminated earth.

A group of men decided to make wooden bakias for
every internee—man, woman, and child—who needed footwear. Children and women were provided first. The soles
were whittled by hand from wood found in camp and were
of original designs. An abandoned automobile tire provided strap material. The flat soled bakia was preferred
for internee use, though Filipino bakias were usually
rounded on the bottom to allow a rolling motion in walking. Interned children as well as adults learned to cup their
toes to hold the bakia upon the foot, and children were
soon able to run while holding the bakia in place, a difficult
accomplishment.

Small rakes and shovels, dolls, blocks, and balls were
hand-made for interned children from tin cans, wood, wrapping string, and animal bones. Both men and women
learned to carve coconut-shell buttons and buckles. Bamboo
was shaped into knitting needles and crocheting hooks for
use with string. Internees also learned to convert bone into
buttons and rings.

When American cigarettes and tobacco were no longer
available, native tobacco products (stronger than American
brands) were bought through the guards. But the rapid
rise in their cost and the difficulty of securing them led to
the trial of tobacco substitutes. One internee before the war

had used tea leaves which had been boiled and redried and, upon his suggestion, as long as tea was available in the camp the used leaves were saved for smokers.

Sun dried papaya leaves and dried grass were rolled in notebook paper. As unnatural as were these cigarette substitutes in appearance and taste, they helped satisfy the tobacco addict. Papaya leaves proved to be the most popular and lasting substitute.

Other substitute materials were also adopted. When toothpaste became exhausted, wood ashes from the outdoor water drums were in great demand as a dentifrice. From an Indian, internees learned to use unraveled socks for sewing thread. Socks from which both heel and toe were worn made useful ravelings, since it was the cuff which was most valuable for this purpose. Attempts to separate dress and shirt materials into thread had been unsuccessful because the threads broke. The Indian pointed out the greater tensile strength of available knitted garments as compared with woven.

Laundering was woman's work. The women not only did their own and their families' washing but also the kitchen towels and the linens for the hospitalized. With the depletion of soap supplies, soapless laundry methods were attempted. Here the Indian came to the rescue again. She contended that clothes could be so well cleansed by the proper use of sun and water that the absence of soap was negligible. The secret of bleaching success, she pointed out, was in keeping the laundry moist so long as it lay exposed to the sun. The following laundry method was widely used in the camp: 1. Soiled clothes were rubbed together in clear water, then rinsed; 2. Wet garments were spread flat upon the grass in the open sunlight; 3. Clothes were sprinkled every half-hour or hour during the day as they became dry; 4. During the full of the moon clothes were left out overnight, flat upon the grass, to benefit from the bleaching and cleansing effects of moonlight and dew.

It was found that a knowledge of the care of animals and fowls, which internees had brought with them into camp, was limited. There were goats, pigs, sheep, rabbits, ducks, chickens, and a carabao. The pigs were of imported stock and had been housed prior to camp purchase in a concrete-floored barn. Unsheltered from tropical rains and heat many became sick and died. The immediate slaughtering of the remainder seemed the only way to prevent this camp investment from becoming a total loss. The men chased the pigs and killed them with sticks and stones. The pigs were then skinned and butchered by amateurs who used ordinary kitchen paring and carving knives. New and unusual cuts appeared, but a minimum of parts was discarded. Other animals were slaughtered and butchered in like manner.

Efforts of the internees to have the guards shoot the camp animals were unsuccessful. Internees, therefore, became adept at stoning, a method also utilized for destroying stray dogs which wandered into camp. Some of the latter were disease carriers; others chased the children and livestock. Piles of stone were always kept handy for this necessary, brutal activity.

Native vegetables which could be expected to grow with a minimum of crop failure were planted, though these proved to be unfamiliar and unpleasant to the American and British palate. Talinum (native spinach) and camotes (sweet potatoes) were selected for the greens which they provided. The camote tops, not the tubers, were consumed.

Careful harvesting of both talinum and camote leaves allowed their continuous reproduction.

Gabi (of the same genus as the American-grown elephant's ear) and a cassava hedge were planted for the nutrient value of their roots. Quick-maturing papaya trees were set out. Unripe papayas were boiled as a vegetable before their more pleasant consumption as a raw fruit was possible. Leeks, corn, beans, ginger, and elongated eggplant grew with moderate success. Cincomas, upo, chayotes—all semitasteless and colorless native foods—responded more successfully to cultivation.

In addition to the serving of the food supplies developed by internees, the camp kitchen also prepared other dishes untested and unknown to the majority of interned men and women. On several occasions the kitchen was able to secure, through purchase from the outside, fresh fish heads. These were for tinola, fish head soup, an inexpensive Filipino delicacy. A small dried fish, dilis, was also available when other foods were not. The dilis was strong in taste and odor and was filled with minute, sharp bones. Carabao meat, from the native work animal, was substituted for imported beef.

The uses of wrapping string during internment were many and varied. In addition to those already mentioned, string was crocheted into belts and hand knitted into socks and underwear for men, women, and children for year-round utility. This emergency material was also utilized by other internees in other parts of the world who found that they could create from wrapping twine articles of beauty as well as usefulness.

A Dutch internee quartered in Württemberg reported

the following employment of string while she was interned, "From the string tied around parcels [sent by the British and American Red Cross and American friends] we made the most ingenious articles—shoes, bags, boxes, ornaments, photograph frames, writing cases, thermos flask covers, and so on. When we desired colored string we just poured boiling water over crinkled colored paper and steeped the string in it. The results were remarkable."[5]

A French internee of the Nazis in France brought to England with her after her release a striking and unusual handbag "quite the smartest one I had seen in England," said a magazine reporter.[6] The ex-internee explained that she had made the bag in a concentration camp in Vittel, France, from string braided together and sewed into a design which formed each side. In exchange for two packages of cigarettes she had had the white string dyed black.

In recognition of the sudden war-time significance of wrapping string in prison camps, the American National Red Cross carried in its *Prisoner of War Bulletin* in 1943 an article entitled "What Can Be Done with String."[7] In this issue of the *Bulletin* (a periodical issued throughout the war for the relatives of American prisoners of war and of civilian internees) it is stated, "Some thirty or forty British women who had been interned at Camp Liebenan in Germany were repatriated this spring. Among their effects were a variety of articles made from string taken from relief parcels. They included tea cozies, letter racks, sprays

[5] Violette C. de Terente, "I Was Interned Forty-Six Months," *Christian Science Monitor Magazine* (December 9, 1944), p. 4.

[6] Neyan W. Stevens, "Out of the Depths," *Independent Woman*, XXIV (1945), 44.

[7] "What Can Be Done with String," American National Red Cross *Prisoner of War Bulletin*, I (1943), 6.

of flowers, shopping baskets, handbags, toy rabbits, a cruet stand, and a toast rack, besides slippers and sandals which, as one internee explained, had come in very useful."[8]

There is general evidence that the internment camp environment fostered the expression of certain practical and ingenious capabilities held latent within men and women by a modern technological civilization.

[8] *Ibid.*

9

Adjustment of Individuals
to the New Culture

DISRUPTIVE effects follow the adoption of any new culture traits. Linton says that a change in the technique connected with the satisfaction of basic biological needs (securing food, shelter, and survival) shakes the very fabric upon which the whole elaborate superstructure of the culture is reared.[1] Linton's observation, based upon studies of primitive cultures, throws light upon the cultural aberrations which occurred within the Bacolod camp. Both the embroideries and the fabric of internees' pre-war culture were altered by internment.

In the Bacolod camp the adoption of new habits was often a painful and an upsetting experience. This was equally true with regard to habit changes resulting from compulsory impact with new materials or new ideas. "I can't stomach the stuff," was commonly heard when tinola, fish head soup, was first served. But in time the attitude toward tinola changed, for internees learned to distinguish between appetite (in which the elements of delight and disgust enter) and hunger (where the psychic values of food lose their meaning).[2]

Likewise, with time and the circumstances of internment internee attitudes toward each other and toward the outside world altered also. Adjustment to the intern-

[1] Ralph Linton, *The Study of Man* (New York: Appleton-Century, 1936), pp. 355-356.
[2] W. B. Cannon, *Bodily Changes in Pain, Hunger, Fear, and Rage* (New York: Appleton, 1916), pp. 233-235.

ment situation was an individual matter, but it followed certain general trends, being influenced by such factors as age, sex, race, and previous socio-economic status of the internees.

During World War I a British doctor, A. L. Vischer, studied the effects of imprisonment upon prisoners of war. He coined the expression "barbed-wire disease" to describe the prisoner's reaction to his prison environment.[3]

In 1944 another British doctor, P. H. Newman, tried to fill in the gaps in the report of Dr. Vischer.[4] He preferred the expression "barbed-wire attitude" to "barbed-wire disease." Dr. Newman described the building up of a new mental attitude by the prisoner of war through four stages: (a) the breaking-in period (the time of acute mental stress which accompanies forcible adaptation to a lower plane of existence); (b) convalescence (the period of recovering of morale and the rearrangement of shattered values); (c) the period of boredom; and (d) the repatriation period. The first two periods of adjustment are of particular interest to the sociologist—i.e., adjustment to the mental stress which accompanies forcible adaptation to a lower level of existence, and rearrangement of shattered values.

As has been pointed out in Chapter 1, most of the published scientific materials relating to the adjustment of transplanted members of society to the prisoner of war experience have been written by and concerned with military, rather than civilian, populations. In his study of the mental

---

[3] A. L. Vischer, *Barbed-Wire Disease, A Psychological Study of the Prisoner of War* (Zurich, 1919). Quoted by P. H. Newman in "The Prisoner-of-War Mentality," *British Medical Journal*, 1 (January, 1944), 8.

[4] P. H. Newman, *op. cit.*

and emotional adjustment of one group of chance associates within a civilian camp, Curt Bondy, formerly professor of social psychology and social pedagogics at the Universities of Hamburg and Göttingen and an inmate of the Buchenwald concentration camp, makes a necessary distinction between (1) prisoners of war, (2) civilian internees, and (3) inmates of refugee camps.[5] He writes, "The internment of prisoners of war is legal; detailed international laws regulate their treatment. The proper execution of these laws is controlled by representatives of neutral states. . . . The prisoners in concentration camps are not legally interned. . . . Inmates of refugee camps are generally people who for racial or political reason have had to leave their countries. Legally the refugee camps must be listed between the war prisoner and the concentration camps." The common, unnerving effect of the indeterminate sentence of war imprisonment of all kinds is pointed out by Bondy.[6]

Dr. Erwin H. Ackerknecht, professor of history of medicine at the University of Wisconsin Medical School, and himself a recent war-time internee in France, has suggested that both prisoner of war camps and concentration camps may be grouped into four categories: (1) routine camps (which provide minimal physical care for the duration of hostilities or until prisoner exchange can be arranged); (2) re-education camps (for the purposes of propagandistic conversion of inmates); (3) slave labor camps; (4) extermination camps. After suggesting this classification,

---

[5] Curt Bondy, "Buchenwald, Germany," *Journal of Abnormal and Social Psychology*, XXXVIII (1943), 453-457.

[6] *Op. cit.* Bondy states that after his war experience his former enthusiasm for the indeterminate sentence for juvenile delinquents has greatly diminished.

Dr. Ackerknecht concludes, "Fundamental traits should be common to all of these camp types."[7]

E. R. C. Walker distinguishes between the frustration which comes with loss of liberty suffered by the civil prisoner and the prisoner of war. Dr. Walker notes that the civil prisoner can hold a grudge against both society and the judge who sent him down. But the prisoner of war has been taught loyalty to his country and his military organization, and so has no one to blame, no scapegoat. "Only a few have the philosophy to accept personal misfortune impersonally," says Dr. Walker.[8]

The psychological and moral influences of war imprisonment have been described by many repatriates, and most seem to agree that social degradation is followed by moral degradation.[9]

The Journal of Social Psychology has printed a most penetrating examination of personality changes during internment. Ija Korner, a trained psychologist, after eleven months in a French internment camp, wrote that *character* differences showed greater constancy than did *emotional* differences of internees.[10]

[7] E. H. Ackerknecht. Letter accompanying unpublished manuscript prepared by Dr. Ackerknecht for the author in February, 1948, concerning his own internee experience during World War II.

[8] E. R. C. Walker, "Impressions of a Repatriated Medical Officer," *Lancet*, 1 (April, 1944), 514.

[9] Curt Bondy, *op. cit.* There has been an outstanding contradiction to Bondy's reports. An interned French journalist writes that prison "comradeship forced each man to develop his more genuine qualities, loyalty and natural generosity." The circumstances of the author's political imprisonment in Tunis, however, were mild in comparison to those in most camps. Philippe Soupalt, *Age of Assassins*, translated by Hannah Josephson (New York: Knopf, 1946), page 211.

[10] Ija Korner, "Psychological Needs of the Individual Dissolving in the Mass and the Possibilities of Clinical Help," *Journal of Social Psychology*, XVI (1942), 143-150.

Korner pointed out that whereas character showed great resistance to mass influence of other internees, emotional responses, on the other hand, followed a new camp clique pattern rather than an individual pattern. Korner also noted that though personalities changed during internment, the relative intelligence levels of internees remained constant.

The above mentioned studies are but a few of the increasing literature relating to the psychological effects of internment.[11]

The individual and his role and status in society are inextricably interwoven. The individual not only acts but *is* a role. Any change in the social scheme which modifies this role may be expected to result in modifications of mental activity and conduct; and a crisis situation such as war internment (which means a sudden uprooting from normal social contacts and a transplanting within a situation of new stimuli and new emphases) requires grave personal adaptation. New social values accompany the internment emphasis upon survival. To these new values each individual finds it necessary to adjust himself within the limits of his own personality—limits of personal variability set by both physiological and social inheritance.

Fortunately, man is a hardy, adaptable animal. "Of all living creatures the human species seems to be the most tenacious of life," a study of internment in France begins. "I was once told by an expert that when parties are lost

[11] See Bibliography of magazine articles and books at end of this manuscript.

in the desert, men are the last to die from thirst or hunger; they survive even camels."[12]

Yet we may assume that being faced with starvation is easier for the camel than for man. Added to the basic survival desire which motivates both, man's urge to come through the experience with his life and his sanity is complicated by acquired cultural anxieties. These concern his prestige, sickness, supernatural or after-life, sex, future security.[13] Certain cultural appetites or combinations of drives (such as the desire for coffee for breakfast and an inclination to starve rather than eat insects) which annoy man in his struggle for survival do not disturb the uncultured camel.

In the Bacolod camp the amenities of life were excluded by internment, and the barrenness, the strenuousness of camp living inevitably resulted in a declining adherence to pre-war culture patterns. Most interned men and women had followed a somewhat orientalized-occidental culture in the Philippines. This culture was based upon (a) wealth and (b) leisure, both of which vanished with the Japanese occupation. The circumstances of internment precluded the performance of many socially correct habits inherent in the pre-war culture pattern.

It is characteristic of man to be mortified by his own personal degeneration. Irwin Edman, the philosopher, has pointed out that,[14] "We are today still horrified by the infringement of a law which, if we stopped to consider it, is

[12] Eleanore Nerac, "Refugee in Internment," *Independent Woman*, XXI (1942), 113.

[13] John Gillin. (Notes from seminar in anthropology, 1945.)

[14] Irwin Edman, *Human Traits and Their Social Significance* (Boston: Houghton Mifflin, 1920), p. 105.

not now, if it ever was, of any genuine service to mankind. . . . Most people's approvals and disapprovals are fixed by what is called 'good taste'; which consists not infrequently in approving what other people approve."

In the Bacolod camp there was knowledge of personal deterioration not only in the individual's own eyes but in the eyes of others as well. This looking-glass self, the reflected personality, is defined by Cooley[15] as having three principal elements: "the imagination of our appearance to the other person, the imagination of his judgment of that appearance, and some sort of self-feeling, such as pride or mortification." Cooley points out that "the thing that moves us to pride or shame is not the mere mechanical reflection of ourselves, but an imputed sentiment, the imagined effect of this reflection upon another's mind."

Jung has described the role of man in his social group as the persona, which he says is[16] "a compromise between the individual and society based on that which one appears to be." But this appearance of man in his social setting, his "identification with office and title has something seductive about it, on which account many men are nothing but the dignity lent them by society." As an example of the danger inherent in the persona Jung describes the professor whose individuality is exhausted by playing the professor's role behind a mask.

CASE STUDY 1

The seductiveness of role, of the persona, was apparent within the Bacolod camp. Corporation executives

---

[15] C. H. Cooley, *Human Nature and the Social Order* (New York: Scribner's, 1920), p. 152.

[16] Jolan Jacobi, *The Psychology of Jung* (New Haven: Yale University Press, 1943), p. 19.

who had enjoyed to the fullest a deep draught of power in the pre-war oriental environment were humiliated by the camp surroundings. They sensed a loss in personal prestige along with the deterioration in the circumstances of their living. To these individuals the superficialities of life *were* life. There was strong emotional reaction when the externalized, material framework upon which their prestige rested collapsed.

The case of Mr. B. illustrates this point. Mr. B. was an executive of a large import concern. His worldliness was couched in superlatives; his staff of household servants was the most numerous, his parties the most lavish, his hobbies the most ostentatious. For its prestige value he imported by plane from Europe fertile pheasant eggs, raised European game birds and served them in lieu of native fowl to his guests.

Mr. B.'s ornate house and his office were both seized during the Japanese occupation. His accumulation of fine Chinese ivories and bronzes, his hand carved furnishings and silver were destroyed. In the mere magnitude of his material disaster he retained a shadow of his former economic prestige.

Several months after the Japanese invasion Mr. B. and his wife were interned. They entered a group in which every man and woman was absorbed with his or her own adjustment problems. Value-attitude systems were shifting rapidly.

Mr. B. was present at the organizational meeting of the Bacolod camp. His self-assurance was unshaken as he sat among the bewildered men, women, and children who gathered to discuss plans for community government. Mr. B. had been able to bring into camp with him rice, camotes, and canned goods sufficient for himself for several months.

Mr. B. remained silent during the recommendation of the Scotsman that personally owned foodstuffs be pooled. Upon nomination of the Scotsman for camp director a former employee of Mr. B. submitted Mr. B.'s name for that position. The first show of hands was so overwhelmingly in favor of the Scotsman that no vote was taken for Mr. B. In similar manner the resolution of the new director for the communal distribution of foodstuffs was adopted.

The popular election of the Scotsman was spontaneous rather than planned, but every day he evidenced more and more the characteristics of leadership sought by internees. Mr. B., on the other hand, assumed the role of a martyr suffering persecution by the camp. He became morose, sullen, and uncooperative in the performance of his assigned tasks.

During the fourth month of internment, when insistent efforts were being made by the director to have the Japanese assume responsibility for feeding the camp, Mr. B. was noticed in frequent conference with the Japanese commandant. The commandant regularly summoned Mr. B. to his office. The latter refused to divulge the subject of their talks, but the relationship between the American and the Japanese seemed to be on a cordial and confidential basis.

Mr. B. was suspected of motivation subversive to the interests of other internees. He was acting in defiance of the internee regulation which forbade communication with the Japanese except with the consent of, or through the person of, the director. Eventually the commandant terminated the series of conferences. But Mr. B. had placed himself under the suspicion of his fellow internees.

Condensed milk, allotted to the camp hospital from pooled supplies, began to disappear from hospital shelves. Mr. B., like other internees, had a turn of duty cleaning hospital quarters and he was suspected of removing the milk. Examination of the garbage near the men's quarters where Mr. B. slept disclosed the recently emptied milk cans. Circumstantial though this evidence was, Mr. B. now stood, in the eyes of the internees, convicted of theft.

An associate of Mr. B. described him before the war as "inventive and constructive in business affairs, independent, industrious, energetic, executive and self-confident." The same associate, after two years of internment with Mr. B., characterized him "motivated solely by personal interests, completely lacking in a proper sense of relative values, evidencing an inability to stand up under disappointment, uncouth."

Mr. B. the successful corporation executive and Mr. B. the internee were seemingly divergent personalities. Yet egocentrism was basic to each. The manner of expression of the ego varied with the situation. Secure in prestige Mr. B. fulfilled adequately the role of economic and social arbiter. Stripped of the externals which made his former prestige possible, Mr. B. illustrates the damaging effects upon human personality of the sudden loss of status and of self-determination.

Mr. B.'s seeming reversal in values was, however, in reality the redirection of pre-existing attitudes upon which the internment situation acted. The new situation appealed to and reinforced certain already established, but otherwise directed, attitudes, emotional habits, and intellectual tendencies.

An army chaplain, endeavoring to explain the apparent personality aberrations observed on the firing lines, has summarized such changes tersely: "Men came out of the war about the same as they went in, only more so."[17]

Linton has discussed the effect upon personality of behavior which is not in accord with a person's established value-attitude system, whatever these value-attitudes may be.[18] "Behavior which is not in accord with the individual's system elicits responses of fear, anger, or at the very least disapproval. . . . Thus an individual who performs an act contrary to one of his own established value-attitude systems will experience considerable emotional disturbance before and after." Many Bacolod internees who felt themselves compelled into action contrary to their pre-war role and its accompanying system of values, and who could not develop new values in keeping with the changed situation, suffered acute emotional disturbance.

Some individuals and groups within the Bacolod camp adjusted themselves to internment more easily than did others. Adjustment is a subjective matter evasive of quantitative measure, but certain objectively determinable factors may be used as a general gauge. Internee medical and death records became a measure of adjustment. Second, participation in the internee-initiated program of the camp afforded a measure of adjustment to camp life. And third, individual behavior in conformity or at variance with the new camp norm indicated a gradation of adjustment or maladjustment to the internment situation.

[17] Eugene Liggett, "Religion," *Time*, XLVI (December 31, 1945), 52.
[18] Ralph Linton, *The Cultural Background of Personality* (New York: Appleton-Century, 1945), pp. 111-113.

Women seemed to adapt themselves to camp life more readily than did male internees. The camp activities of women were not so far removed from their pre-war roles and experiences as were the camp duties of men. Interned women prepared camp food, cared for interned children and the sick, looked after the camp laundry. The situation was new to the women; the activities and the domestic role they represented were not entirely so.

Interned men, on the other hand, found their days filled with actions both unfamiliar and repulsive to them. The cleaning of outdoor toilets, the burying of garbage, cutting of grass and weeds, left the men's bodies weary and their minds and ambitions thwarted. Financial and business worries preyed heavily upon the men. In addition, man's prestige in the role of protector of women and children suffered by his internment. He was humiliated by the compulsory taking of orders from the Japanese in the presence of wife and friends.

The easier camp adjustment of women was apparently due to the social and cultural characteristics of the two sexes, as well as to biological differences. The traditional self-sacrifice and resignation expected of women aided them in the internment situation.[19]

Both men and women who could not adjust to camp life "cracked-up." The preponderance of crack-ups among male internees is illustrated in a summary of the sex distribution of illnesses resulting in death within the larger camp of Santo Tomas into which Bacolod internees were absorbed in March, 1943. Most of these deaths occurred during the second and third years of internment,

[19] For a pertinent discussion see Mabel A. Elliott and F. E. Merrill, *Social Disorganization* (New York: Harper's, 1941), pp. 551-552.

available statistical information on Santo Tomas reveals.[20]

In Santo Tomas the daily ration of food was the same for men and women, though men assigned to heavy duty such as cutting wood and hauling camp supplies were provided extra food while performing these tasks. Living conditions were the same for both sexes. Yet, in a population 61 per cent male, of deaths by illness (exclusive of deaths resulting from Japanese torture and enemy shelling) 89.5 per cent were male. The female population (39 per cent of the total) suffered only 10.5 per cent of deaths from illness.[21] Both of the two recorded suicides were male. Men were somewhat older than women, but age differences cannot account for the wide variation in death ratios of the sexes.

Records of adult weight changes in the Santo Tomas camp indicate greater actual and greater percentage weight loss among men than women.[22] The adult weight losses totaled 70,000 pounds, or 35 tons. Five men lost more than 100 pounds each. One woman lost 95 pounds, none more than that. The weights of children were not included in the camp survey upon which the figures in Table vii are based, for a failure of a child to gain was the equivalent of a weight loss to an adult.

The minor adjustments faced by women due to feminine vanity should be mentioned. A case in point is that of an internee who had dyed her hair, unknown to her friends, for some years prior to the war. Interned without dyeing preparations she bound her head in a kerchief for several

[20] F. H. Stevens, *Santo Tomas* (New York: Stratford House, 1946); and J. E. McCall, *Santo Tomas Internment Camp* (Lincoln, Nebraska: Woodruff Co., 1945).

[21] See Tables v and vi.

[22] Table vii.

TABLE V

Number and Per cent, by Age and Sex,
of Santo Tomas Camp Population
August 31, 1943*

| | TOTAL | | Men | | Women | |
	No.	Per cent	No.	Per cent	No.	Per cent
TOTAL	6,874	100.0	4,203	61.1	2,671	38.9
Through 7 yrs.	667	9.5	329	7.8	338	12.6
8-17 yrs.	607	9.0	343	8.1	264	9.9
18-59 yrs.	4,374	63.5	2,588	61.6	1,786	66.9
60-69 yrs.	948	14.0	723	17.2	225	8.4
70 yrs. & over	278	4.0	220	5.3	58	2.2

* These figures include approximately 2,100 internees (men, women, and children) later transferred from Santo Tomas to Los Baños camp, also on Luzon Island. Age groupings are from J. E. McCall's *Santo Tomas Internment Camp*, p. 66. Death statistics are from the same source, pp. 137-146, checked by information in F. H. Stevens' *Santo Tomas*, pp. 487-569, and mimeographed material distributed within Santo Tomas camp.

TABLE VI

Number and Per cent, by Age and Sex,
of Deaths by Disease in Santo Tomas Camp,
January, 1942 to March, 1945*

| | TOTAL | | Men | | Women | |
	No.	Per cent	No.	Per cent	No.	Per cent
TOTAL	362	100.0	324	89.5	38	10.5
Through 7 yrs.	8	2.2	5	1.5	3	7.9
8-17 yrs.	2	.6	2	.6	0	0
18-59 yrs.	101	27.9	81	25.0	20	52.6
60-69 yrs.	142	39.2	133	41.1	9	23.7
70 yrs. & over	109	30.1	103	31.8	6	15.8

* These figures include approximately 2,100 internees (men, women, and children) later transferred from Santo Tomas to Los Baños camp, also on Luzon Island. Age groupings are from J. E. McCall's *Santo Tomas Internment Camp*, p. 66. Death statistics are from the same source, pp. 137-146, checked by information in F. H. Stevens' *Santo Tomas*, pp. 487-569, and mimeographed material distributed within Santo Tomas camp.

TABLE VII

Changes in Weight, by Age and Sex,
of Adult Internees in Santo Tomas Camp,
January, 1945*

	19-40 years			41-60 years			Over 60 years		
	Total	M	F	Total	M	F	Total	M	F
Total no. internees	1,175	508	667	1,003	555	448	560	433	119
Av. normal wt., pounds	143	166	125	157	175	135	171	177	149
Av. weight Jan., 1945	111	124	101	112	122	100	114	119	96
Av. pounds loss	32	42	24	45	53	35	57	58	53

SUMMARY OF TABLE VII

	TOTAL	Male	Female
Total no. internees	2,738	1,506	1,232
Av. normal wt., pounds	154	172	132
Av. weight Jan., 1945	112	121	100
Av. pounds loss	42	51	32

* Changes in internee weights from statistical information in McCall's *Santo Tomas Internment Camp*, p. 96, and Stevens' *Santo Tomas*, pp. 125-126.

months in an effort to conceal the increasing grayness near her scalp. Unable to continue the deception—due to the lack of privacy for washing her hair or for tieing the turban in her sleeping quarters—the woman turned her former vanity into a joke. She laughed about the age which she had attempted unsuccessfully to conceal. With the discarding of the artifices of youth, the frankly aging woman spoke of a daughter in college outside the Islands. Before the war she had been ashamed to acknowledge her child, for the daughter's age was a clue to her own.

Men, women, and children who had lived with Filipinos and had adopted Island habits found internment less difficult than did those who had held themselves aloof from the Island culture. The American or Britisher who had transplanted himself and his family to the tropics and had then sent back to his homeland for all the accustomed foods and other amenities of foreign life found the conditions within the camp almost unbearable. To these the adoption of new food and living habits was emotionally as well as gastronomically upsetting.

Being faced with a bowl of tinola—a clear soup in which a wide-eyed fish head floated—caused some foreigners to leave the dining room with nausea. Philippinized men, women, and children consumed the tinola with relish. Also difficult for foreigners to eat was the Philippine dried dilis fish. Few in the islands, except Filipinos, had eaten carabao meat before internment. To ease the acceptance of this meat by foreigners, it was introduced in a stew in which the other ingredients partially killed the real or imagined horsy taste.

Rice three times a day upset digestions not accustomed to its starchiness and bulk. While acute gas pains were suffered by internees unfamiliar with rice as a primary food supply, those already adjusted to it complained of the inadequacy of the food rather than its kind. Internees hospitalized with dietary disturbances were not those who had followed the native way of life. On the contrary, they were those who had been most meticulous in their selection of imported food products.

Experience in Filipino home life, which often included grandparents, uncles, aunts, and other relatives as members of the family, also made internment easier. In such households privacy was not only lacking but was seemingly undesired. But to the American or Britisher who considered privacy as essential to his well being and as his inalienable foreign prerogative, the adjustment to camp living arrangements was trying. The physical discomfort suffered by Americans and British as a result of the loss of foreign household furnishings was also not shared by the Philippinized internee who brought with him into camp the mat upon which he slept at home.

In still another manner those who had followed Island habits were at an advantage during internment. The emphasis of tropical cultures upon the benefits of today rather than the possible losses or gains of tomorrow permitted Philippinized internees an enviable freedom of mind.

It would be difficult to separate the mental from the physical distress which descended upon foreign men when their livelihood was cut off. The loss of present comforts, however, was not so frightening as the fear of the future. The destruction of Island sugar and lumber mills meant that almost two-thirds of the internee heads of families in the Bacolod camp would be without employment after the war. The Japanese expropriation of boats, barges, and piers caused internee executives of an inter-Island shipping company to be apprehensive about their positions after the war.

It was estimated that three years would be required to rebuild a sugar central, replant cane fields, and have ready for export the finished sugar product. To the large group dependent upon the sugar industry the future looked dark indeed. They knew, also, that post-war plans for Philippine sugar were further complicated by the Island political situation. Philippine independence might make rebuilding unfeasible.

The operation of Negros mills was generally based upon twenty year contracts with cane growers. Many of these contracts, signed around 1923, would expire before the end of the war. Unless long-term tax and tariff arrangements could be made with the independent Island government as the groundwork for new long-term contracts with planters, the sugar centrals would not be reopened. Anxiety for their future economic well being deeply depressed former members of sugar central staffs, many of whom considered themselves out of jobs.

The most acute anxiety was felt by those with fewest employable years ahead. Men past fifty with long Island experience which did not fit them for American occupations were the most harassed by fear of the future.[23]

In contrast to the apprehension of Bacolod commercial groups concerning their futures was the serene attitude of

[23] In this connection there is an interesting commentary upon the reactions to military imprisonment of different age groups: "It seemed . . . that of those who were impressed and oppressed by the German success, the greatest proportion were in their thirties. The older men had seen and taken part in the smashing of the German military machine before, and were for the most part convinced that there was no essential reason why this should not happen again. The younger men, too, seemed to have more faith. It was among the middle group that one found the 'realists' who regarded their elders as 'dead-beats' given over to wishful thinking and juniors as irresponsible youngsters. Can this phenomenon be associated with adolescence in the disillusioned 1920's? Or is it that the dislocating effect is greater on the man but recently started on his career?" E. R. C. Walker, "Impressions of a Repatriated Medical Officer," *Lancet*, 1 (April, 1944), 514.

missionaries and priests. The churches which supported them were unharmed by the war. Post-war positions were assured. To some their future was enhanced by the war experience, for imprisonment in line of duty would elevate them in the eyes of the church. With an assurance of manner lacking in the other men and women, the missionaries and priests went about the performance of their daily camp tasks.

The outstanding instance of absence of strain—and one might say, the presence of joy—during internment was exemplified by an American priest. A teacher in a Filipino boys' school in Cebu City (Cebu Island) at the outbreak of war, the priest, Father Millan, had come to Negros only slightly ahead of the Japanese. He had remained in Cebu until that city was demolished in April, 1942. He had then hidden in the woodlands near by until he and a Filipino boy found opportunity of crossing the narrow channel to Negros. They came at night in a native boat. The father brought to Negros with him only "a mass kit, chalice from Mary Knoll, stone from the Archbishop Reyes, vestments from a woman's circle in Detroit, and wine from the stock of the Army."[24]

Father Millan also brought with him a firm conviction to make the best of the war experience—a conviction which resulted in his introducing into the camp an organized recreation program. His insistent efforts to divert internee energies from worry to play helped many an internee avoid mental breakdown.

Varied incentives had brought the American men and

[24] R. E. Sheridan, *Recollections of Four Years, 1941-1945.* (Published for private circulation. La Salle College, Manila, P.I., 1945), p. 7.

women interned on Negros to the Philippines. A few of the men had come out with the American Army (at the time of the Spanish-American War) and had remained after a tour of duty. These "old timers" had not infrequently married Filipino wives. But most of the American men had come to Negros because of the lucrative positions which were open. Not only were salaries and percentages of profit higher than for similar endeavors in the States, but added perquisites made work in the Philippines attractive. A furnished home, an automobile and chauffeur, and an entertainment allowance were extra inducements which accompanied offers to white foreigners. The car and driver were for face as well as necessity.[25]

The unmarried white women who were living on Negros at the outbreak of war had come for less tangible reasons. Without exception they were teachers or missionaries employed in fields in which income was not the main appeal. These women had come most often as the result of the desire for new experience in the tropics or because of firm religious conviction. The background of an active participant in camp affairs—a woman who had come to the Islands originally as an unmarried teacher and had married there—will illustrate the urge which had prompted her and others to break away from United States' boundaries.

CASE STUDY 2

Marian was a small, supercharged dynamo during the whole of internment. She was five feet tall and weighed a hundred pounds when she entered camp. Brown eyed, gray haired, she was still attractive despite a quarter-century of

[25] This point is emphasized by the American Internees Committee in claims filed for car losses in the Philippines. *Bulletin of the American Internees Committee* (San Francisco, March 28, 1946).

teaching in America and the Islands. Marian's determination to distinguish herself began at her high school graduation.

In Marian's high school senior play each student was shown being fed, as a freshman, into a complicated grinding machine from which he emerged as a finished product. The professors who turned the handle of the mill found grinding difficult for some students. The gears jammed with algebra books as a boy passed slowly through. Love letters and dance programs almost brought the mill to a stop for a girl. But when Marian went into the hopper, with one turn of the handle she appeared a senior, having passed all cogs without difficulty. The comment of the play announcer was: "She is so little; she is so quiet; she is so easy to educate."

Marian rebelled at being taken for granted. At the age of seventeen she applied for a job as principal of a school with six teachers, and was accepted. After later completion of college training and varied United States teaching experience Marian struck out for wider fields. Through the Bureau of Education in Washington she secured free transportation to the Philippines and a contract for work in Island schools. She chose to teach in isolated villages where she could learn the native customs rather than to live in the foreign communities of the Islands. She wrote and published many stories of Philippine life. While teaching she met and married an executive of one of the sugar centrals.

The Bacolod camp afforded Marian further opportunities for self-expression. It was she who opened a camp library after cataloging books found in the Bacolod school and other books brought in by internees. Marian utilized the camp as an experimental laboratory for testing the pedagogical hypothesis that measurable progress in elementary reading and writing is not retarded by the use of bilingualism. The advances of internee children Marian taught from hand prepared English-Spanish texts defended her bilingual educational theory.

Forming a distinct group within the Bacolod camp were the American women married to Filipinos. Peculiarly individual circumstances had surrounded each such marriage. The women were from Louisiana, Indiana, New York, and Texas; three of them had met their future husbands in the United States; the fourth had married a Filipino doctor after working with him in the Islands.

The youngest of the American women married to a Filipino was the daughter of an administrative officer of a well known American Catholic University who had studied with her husband while he was in the United States. After his graduation, the Filipino had returned to his Island hacienda and the girl had flown to Negros to be married. At the outbreak of war she lived in a remote agricultural section of Negros where she shared the companionship of her husband's Filipino and Spanish relatives.

A second interned American wife of a Filipino was also college trained. Her husband, executive of a sugar central, had met her while on a business trip to the States. A third American wife had been a waitress prior to her marriage. She and her Filipino husband had enjoyed in the United States an interracial, bohemian society before going to the Islands to live. The fourth American wife of a Filipino was graduated from an American nursing school. She met her future husband while she was on the staff of an Island mission hospital.

The American men, as well as women, who had married Filipinos found their Island life closely allied with that of Filipino relatives and friends. They had, after marriage, looked to them for social contacts rather than to white society.

In summary it may be said that cultural and racial characteristics accentuated or retarded adjustment to Bacolod camp life, since the basic personality structure[26] of the occidental and the Filipino differed. There were also personal deviations within each national and cultural group, the Americanized Filipinos and the Philippinized Americans falling between the two extremes of occidental and oriental personality structures. The Filipino lack of concern for the future,[27] independence of the need for privacy, and acquiescence to fate (an attitude reminiscent of the generations of Spanish subjugation and its accompanying Catholicism) eased the strain of internment for followers of the native culture. The culture of western man offered no such palliatives to its interned adherents.

The tyranny of reality was too great for some internees. There were a few notable evidences of day dream-

---

[26] "Basic personality . . . is merely the name for a diagnostic summary of the constellations existing in a given society." . . . "The term *basic personality structure* was chosen to obviate the lack of clarity in the terms group, national, or social character." Abram Kardiner, *The Psychological Frontiers of Society* (New York: Columbia University Press, 1945), pp. xvii and 24.

[27] Porteus emphasizes the interest of the Filipino in the immediate present in his study of the Hawaiians, Chinese, Japanese, Portuguese, and Filipinos in Hawaii. S. D. Porteus and Marjorie Babcock. *Temperament and Race* (Boston: Richard Badger Co., 1926).

ing and phantasy as efforts at escape. The experience of Bacolod internees in this respect was repeated in a camp in Tunis, though there is no evidence that the dreams in the widely separated camps followed the same patterns. Soupalt writes, "Dreams were not only an escape—they were life on a larger plane, more free even than life outside of the prison. None of them (the prisoners) struggled against it; they all abandoned themselves voluptuously to the current that led to the unknown."[28]

The first necessary step in the adjustment of both men and women to internment was a facing of the facts. As long as this was avoided adjustment was impossible; once this was accomplished, a major hurdle was overcome. Woodworth has summarized this in the following statement: "A person remains unadjusted to a state of affairs if he has not sensed it, or if the facts though new have left no impression on him, or if he dislikes the situation and is unwilling to take the appropriate action. He may be unready to act because he does not want to act. His dislike and unwillingness may even prevent him from seeing the situation as it is and so lead to maladjustment."[29]

In summary it may be noted that when faced with the Bacolod internment situation individuals reacted variously. Such reactions were modified by both physiological and cultural inheritance. But, apparently, more influential than the biological factors of sex, age, and race, were the pre-war cultural patterns to which the individuals had adhered.

[28] Soupalt, *op. cit.*
[29] Robert S. Woodworth, *Adjustment and Mastery* (Baltimore: Williams and Wilkins, 1933), p. 55.

A Community under Stress

"Catastrophes are great educators of mankind," wrote Sorokin[1] in his study of the calamitous effects of famine, pestilence, war, and revolution upon human mental life and social organization.

Man has learned much about himself from both historical and contemporary observation of human action in time of stress. Calamity on a personal basis or on a nationwide scale is disturbing to the emotions and thoughts of those within its range of influence. Sorokin notes in detail how calamities affect the cognitive processes, the desires, and the volitions of those faced with them.[2] He notes the concentration of the cognitive processes (sensation and perception, attention, association of images and flow of ideas, dreams, memory, and reproductive imagination) upon the phenomena that are directly or indirectly connected with the calamity and the incapacity to concentrate on objects unrelated to it.

In the field of desires, wishes, will, and volition Sorokin points out that the principal change brought about by calamities consists in a reinforcement of the desires and wishes directed toward the mitigation of sufferings imposed by the calamity. There is a corresponding weakening or elimination of all contrary desires and wishes.

Alexander H. Leighton, psychiatrist and cultural anthropologist, published in 1945 a critical analysis of the

---

[1] P. A. Sorokin, *Man and Society in Calamity* (New York: Dutton and Company, 1942), p. 10.

[2] Sorokin, *op. cit.*, Chapter II, "How Calamities Affect Our Cognitive Processes, Desires, and Volitions," pp. 27-47.

struggle of Japanese men, women, and children in the United States to mitigate the effects of a wholly unnatural cultural situation created for them by the calamity of World War II.[3] Uprooted from their homes on the west coast these individuals were transferred en masse to relocation centers. Certain types of human stress became evident as Leighton observed the evacuated Japanese in their relation to their new physical and social environment.

Problems faced by the Japanese within the relocation centers and by internees within the Bacolod camp were similar in many ways. The same types of stress—in greater or less degree—were evidenced in both situations. These stresses were the outcome of the thwarting of both basic and acquired, or cultural, drives. Threats to life and health, physical discomfort, and deprivation of sexual satisfaction which resulted from the mass confinement of individuals interfered with basic human motivations. On the other hand, the withdrawal from the individual of his means of gaining a livelihood, his enforced idleness, and the unpredictable behavior of those in positions of dominance over him in the new social order resulted, in the Bacolod camp, in stresses largely of cultural determination. As widespread as are these latter desires and expectations they do not characterize in like degree all cultures of mankind. The free enterprise system of America and the pre-war neo-democracy of the Philippines were particularly antithetic of these repressions.

Guided by Leighton's general outline[4] the following types of stress may be described within the Bacolod camp:

[3] A. H. Leighton, *The Governing of Men* (Princeton: Princeton University Press, 1946).

[4] Leighton, *op. cit.*, p. 252.

1. *Threats to life and health.* Early apprehension of death from assault by the camp guards was replaced in the Bacolod camp with later fear of death from starvation or disease. The threats to life were at some stages more imagined than real, but the suffering was none the less acute, for "a feeling of threat can be in itself a dynamic stimulation to other reactions."[5]

Added to the basic desire to live was anxiety about the future well being of dependents in case of death. Such an anxiety—a deviation from the basic drive to continue life—was a strong occidental cultural force.

2. *Discomfort from pain, heat, cold, dampness, fatigue, and poor food.* Physical discomfort characterized the entire period of Bacolod internment. Poorly prepared and inadequate food, overcrowding, the absence of chairs and comfortable beds, exposure to tropical sun and rain caused bodily pain and mental disturbance. Continual thwarting of the basic drive for comfort resulted in cumulative physical and mental fatigue and in undue irritability.

3. *Loss of means of subsistence, whether in the form of money, jobs, business, or property.* Added to the actual suffering caused internees by the loss of essential foods and clothing was anxiety as to how these and other material losses might affect post-war status and security. Often culturally determined anxieties concerning the future crowded out more veritable threats in the present.

4. *Deprivation of sexual satisfaction.* The type of casual, non-sexual association which the Japanese permitted husbands and wives interned together in Bacolod was unsatisfying. Yet husbands and wives completely isolated by the war

[5] A. H. Maslow, "Conflict, Frustration and the Theory of Threat," *Journal of Abnormal and Social Psychology*, XXXVIII (1943), 81-86.

suffered far greater sexual deprivation, in the broader im-
plications of lack of affection. The full significance of the
enforced absence from members of the other sex for whom
affectional attachments had been formed has been pointed
out with reference to military prisoners of war: "There can
be little doubt," wrote a released prisoner[6] in the *British
Medical Journal*, "that in the broader sense of lack of affection, sexual deprivation is not only fundamental but *the*
fundamental factor in the formation of the prisoner of war
attitude. Deeply within the prisoner, but seldom expressed,
there lies the fear of becoming a forgotten man."

The sexual anxieties which loomed large in the mind of
the American prisoner of war were also present within the
civilian male separated by internment from his spouse. A
fear of infidelity on the part of wives and sweethearts is a
widespread anxiety among men brought up in our culture.[7]

5. *Enforced idleness.* Though there were no periods of
enforced idleness in the Bacolod camp the camp activities
were not satisfying. The goal of day-by-day subsistence
failed to call forth the efforts and enthusiasms of pre-war
long range incentives.

6. *Restriction of movement.* Restriction of movement
and communication resulted in restriction of thought and
speech. Internees tended to become conversational postverts
(as contrasted with anteverts) with emphasis upon the past.
The monotony of internment encouraged representational
expressions concerning completed activities as an effort to
satisfy the thwarted desires for new experience.

Another aspect of limited movement was the absence of
privacy. Some cultures permit almost no privacy (Pueblo,

[6] P. H. Newman, *op. cit.*

[7] Kimball Young, "Population and Power: Some Comments on Demographic Changes in Europe," *Social Forces*, xxv (1946), 6.

Filipino) but they do permit freedom of movement and have an adequately regulated social life. Within the Bacolod camp freedom of movement, a regulated social life, and privacy were all lacking. There was no opportunity of isolating oneself from other persons and the forced awareness of the petty details of others' lives. There was an absence of the minimum of privacy which some cultures deem essential to keeping the ego intact. A British repatriate from a World War I prisoner of war camp in East Africa has reported, "To some of us the discomforts of being always, day and night, in a crowd, and a noisy crowd at that, was perhaps even more unpleasant than the actual hardships we had to endure at times."[8] And an American civilian internee living in Borneo under conditions similar to those in Bacolod writes: "The most deteriorating factor was the complete lack of privacy in camp."[9]

Irwin Edman, the philosopher, places great emphasis upon the importance of privacy in modern life. Edman summarizes his belief as follows: "Just as man can be satiated with too much eating, and irritated by too much activity, so men become 'fed up' with companionship. The demand for solitude and privacy is thus fundamentally a physiological demand, like the demand for rest. . . . Companionship, even the most desirable kind, exhausts nervous energy, and may become positively fatiguing and painful. . . . A normal life demands a certain proportion of solitude just as much as it demands the companionship of others."[10]

[8] E. F. Spanton, *In German Gaols* (London: Society for Promoting Christian Knowledge, 1917), p. 63.

[9] Agnes N. Keith, "All Are Guilty," *Atlantic Monthly*, CLXXVIII (1946), 43.

[10] Irwin Edman, *Human Traits and Their Social Significance* (Boston: Houghton Mifflin Company, 1920), p. 138.

Edman concludes that privacy is also necessary as a matter of "emotional protection in individuals in whom there is a highly sensitive development of personal selfhood."[11] He notes that children love to have secrets and older people often feel a sense of irritation at having their personal affairs and feelings displayed.

As has been pointed out, within the Bacolod camp the loss of personal privacy was an aspect of restriction of movement particularly oppressive to American and British cultural groups.

7. *Isolation.* Isolation is listed by Leighton as one of the causes of human stress. Bacolod internees were isolated from their own groups of pre-war voluntary associates, but there was no isolation of individual from individual within the camp.

8. *Threats to children, family members, and friends.* Internees with family members and friends separated from them were afflicted with particular anxieties. However, the war-time cessation of income caused acute distress to all internee heads of families with adults or children dependent upon them and for whom they could no longer provide. Not only were these men unable to continue financial responsibilities but they were also denied the giving of physical protection to those who looked to them for it.

9. *Rejection, dislike, and ridicule from other people.* "Ridicule will bring almost any individual to terms, while the most stubborn rebel will bow before ostracism or the threat of expulsion from his group."[12] Japanese in relocation centers in the United States were a minority subject to

[11] *Op. cit.*, p. 139.
[12] Ralph Linton, *The Study of Man*, pp. 141-142.

public ridicule and scorn. Philippine internees, on the other hand, had the sympathy of the outside majority. Ridicule became a means of social control within the Bacolod camp. It was utilized by the larger internee group to hold would-be nonconformists to adherence to camp policies.

10. *Capricious and unpredictable behavior on the part of those in authority and upon whom one's welfare depends.* The unpredictable activities of the Japanese in control of the Bacolod camp have been discussed fully in Chapter 7. An expectation that those in positions of dominance would follow certain behavior patterns (which they did not) was evidenced by the evacuated Japanese as well as by internees in the Philippines. It would be interesting to know if the expectations differed as widely as the actualities in the two situations.

Leighton pointed out the influence of the above mentioned types of stress upon Japanese within relocation centers in the United States. The following additional disturbing factors, not listed by Leighton, affected all or some of the Bacolod internees:

11. *Subjection to enemy propaganda.* Internees in Bacolod were subjected to a persistent Japanese propaganda program. General facts concerning progress of the war were not only withheld from internees but the discussion of the war by internees in their private conversation was forbidden. The only type of reading material provided by the Japanese related through cartoons and anecdote the misdeeds and inefficiency of the white man in the Far East. Typical of such material was that in the Japanese controlled Hong Kong *News,* which on January 14, 1942, carried the statement, "The vaunted supermen of the white race have

melted like butter."[13] This was part of a scheme to swing orientals into cooperation with the Japanese, and the widespread acceptance of such statements accelerated the personal degeneration already caused by conditions of internment.

12. *Awareness of personal degeneration.* Within the Bacolod camp men and women ate with their fingers and with spoons because there were insufficient knives and forks; they failed to bathe because of the uncertainty and inadequacy of the water supply; they screamed at children and at each other because they were too tired to move near enough for normal conversational tones. Among the women there was the known impairment of personal beauty and physical attractiveness.

As has been noted, internment compelled men and women to perform acts contrary to their own established values and to witness other people's acts which were contrary to such values. Thus emotional responses were elicited when the individual was not threatened in any way.

Linton has pointed out the strong reactions of Americans who witness certain customs in Latin countries which are not in agreement with the visitors' values of sanitation and modesty.[14] The American who would be pained at the sight of the South American excreting in public responded unhappily to the internment camp custom of publicly picking food particles from carious teeth. The latter act was emotionally disturbing whether performed in the American's presence or performed, contrary to his values, by himself.

[13] R. S. Ward, *Asia for the Asiatics?* (Chicago: University of Chicago Press, 1945), p. 44.
[14] Ralph Linton, *Cultural Background of Personality*, pp. 111-113.

In concluding his study of the types of stress Leighton lists certain general types, derived from the more specific types already mentioned, which give force to the specific. These general, or derived types of stress are: (1) persistent frustration of goals, desires, needs, intentions, and plans; (2) circumstances that promote the dilemma of conflicting and mutually incompatible desires and intentions; (3) circumstances creating confusion and uncertainty as to what is happening in the present and what can be expected in the future.[15]

Circumstances within the Bacolod camp generated frustration, disorientation and dilemma. Though these derived stresses characterize to a certain degree all of human society, within the Bacolod camp these stresses became sufficiently disturbing as to be subversive to the normal dictates of both basic and culturally acquired drives. One factor contributing to disorientation and dilemma in Bacolod and which has not been discussed fully was rumor.

The effects of rumor in both the relocation centers and in the Bacolod camp should be pointed out. Anxieties in the relocation centers associated with feelings of insecurity formed a fertile field for alarmist rumors.[16] Such anxieties were also present in Bacolod. Would the Bacolod internees remain in Bacolod or be moved elsewhere? Would the Japanese begin to feed the internees or were American Red Cross supplies on the way? If the war lasted another year what would happen to the sick? Would the American gov-

---

[15] Leighton, *op. cit.*, p. 260.

[16] John F. Embree, "Causes of Unrest at Relocation Centers," *Community Analysis Report No. 2*. U.S. Department of the Interior, War Relocation Authority (Washington, D.C., 1943), p. 1.

ernment reimburse internees for their property losses?
Why was no mail permitted in the camp?

Anxieties about food, health, the duration of the war,
grew as particular incidents focused attention upon one or
the other of these. A particularly lean meal resulted in rumors of confiscation by the Japanese of the pooled food
supplies. A case of severe illness was followed by rumors
of a camp-wide disease epidemic. The circulation by the
Japanese commandant of reports of new Japanese military
successes caused rumors of a five-year or ten-year war. Each
unpleasant event became a new source of fear and rumor.
Within the Bacolod camp, as in relocation centers in the
United States, "the uncertainties of the new life and the intense concern about present and future welfare led to the
construction of a shifting and fanciful world of additional
uncertainties and distorted human relationships, to more
fears, and to further distrust."[17] From a study of rumors in
the American Armed Forces during World War II it was
discovered that the most important single factor related to
the frequency and the extent of diffusion of rumors was the
total amount of non-rumored information in circulation at
the time.[18] In their thorough analysis of rumor, Allport
and Postman also found a definite pattern of distortion.[19]

Rumor had its lighter side. The fabrication of wholly
unreliable and humorous rumors often served as a means
of breaking the monotony of daily living. Such rumors gave

[17] *United States Department of the Interior*, War Relocation Authority,
"Impounded People, Japanese Americans in the Relocation Centers"
(Washington, D.C., 1947), p. 65.
[18] Theodore Caplow, "Rumors in War," *Social Forces*, xxv (1947),
300.
[19] G. W. Allport and Leo Postman, *The Psychology of Rumor* (New
York: Henry Holt & Co., 1947).

a zest to camp life and provided an inexhaustible subject for conversation when other themes were lacking.

Children and young people within the Bacolod camp had their own special problems. Camp life affected the mental as well as the social life of young children. With a paucity of playthings the small children tended to hoard and cache in their quarters or about the grounds what few toys they could find or create. *Things* became all important.

Child psychologists have pointed out the naturally possessive relation of the infant to objects which he has acquired. At about five years the child begins to take personal pride in *his* belongings,[20] a tendency of children to acquisitive behavior which seemed accentuated by the inadequately defined property lines within the camp. What was *mine* to one child—e.g., stones, bottles, and empty tin cans found upon the grounds—was frequently the basis of dispute with another child or his parents. It was not practicable to hold all gratuitous and discarded items as the property of all the children. The impartial enforcement of such a policy would have required more adult time than could be allotted to it. Each child, therefore, attempted to mark or have marked for him every piece of glass, wood, string, or stone which he wished to add to his personal collection.

Children under six years indicated in their nomenclature and in their play a war influence. When built up stones or blocks toppled they had been "bombed." "Kill" and "murder" were glibly uttered by the very young, usually with

[20] Arnold Gesell and Frances Ilg, *The Child from Five to Ten* (New York: Harper's, 1946), p. 24.

reference to dolls, stuffed animals, and other inanimate objects.

Anna Freud, who studied the actions of children in nurseries and kindergartens in England during the bombings there, noted that "When adults go over their experiences in conscious thought and speech, children do the same in their play."[21] Miss Freud noticed that during the war London children ceased playing train and played aeroplane; the noise of trains became that of flying planes. The British children "bombed" their toy houses with bricks.

The fact that all young Bacolod children—with the exception of an infant whose mother had died at its birth—continued throughout the duration of the camp in association with their own mothers doubtless prevented the mental maladjustments which might otherwise have coincided with a lack of home life during the first five years.

What children believed about conditions under which they lived was more important than the actual conditions. Realizing this, value-attitudes were deliberately patterned for children by their parents. The reactions of young Bacolod internees to the presence of Japanese guards, to the shortage of food, to the material and space restrictions imposed upon them became, therefore, childish expressions of attitudes selected by adults because of (1) the expediency of the attitude, or (2) the permanent effect of the attitude upon the child's later thinking.

(1) Respect and consideration for the authority of the Japanese were instilled into children by parents who themselves feared, hated, and distrusted the Japanese. It was expedient to acknowledge bowing as a solemn recognition

---

[21] Anna Freud and Dorothy T. Burlingham, *War and Children* (New York: Medical War Books, 1943), p. 67.

of Japanese dominance. Failure of the toddler to bend from his waist might result in confiscation by the Japanese of essential food supplies.

(2) Prejudice against all Japanese because they were members of a different race was, in general, discouraged in children by their parents. Such action grew out of the realization that by teaching hatred of the racially different Japanese the groundwork could be laid inadvertently for the cultivation of prejudice against all groups physically or culturally unlike the children themselves. Parents guarded their speech in the presence of children. It was sensed that adult hatreds and fears might permanently affect the character of the interned child by leading to frustration and vindictive behavior on the part of the child.

Camp discipline was severe. Children were forbidden by the Japanese to enter certain areas where the lawns were tempting for play. The children did not intrude, though no fences marked the out-of-bounds areas. Unbroken silence was demanded of children during the daily two hour siesta. Children stood at attention through long roll calls and inspections. However, unless the child became overtired by the physical demands made upon him, the disciplinary regulations were not in themselves harmful. Of greater significance were the reaction patterns of the children to the camp discipline.

The Japanese were not unaware of the role of parents in the formation of attitudes expressed by interned children. Mothers were at all times held responsible by the Japanese for the speech as well as actions of their children. In Santo Tomas a mother was slapped by the commandant when her four-year-old daughter was overheard to refer to a guard as a "Jap"—a forbidden brevity. The mother was warned that she would be punished more severely if the daughter used offensive language again.

There was no blunting of the sensitivity of children in the Bacolod and Santo Tomas camps by scenes of cruelty and death such as occurred in European civilian camps. Instances of public torture were rare and restricted almost wholly to the last few months of the war. Unpleasant encounters between internees and Japanese, and between adult internees, were, whenever possible, kept from the sight and knowledge of children. The fact that the children lived in segregated quarters facilitated such endeavors.

American five- and six-year-olds who spent three years in internment in the Philippines found it necessary to make minor adjustments when they entered United States kindergartens and first grades after release. They were unacquainted with animals usually seen by children in picture books, zoos, and circuses. Interned children were also unfamiliar with folk stories and fairy tales which are a part of the American cultural initiation of the very young. A knowledge of American monetary symbols and values was lacking.

Undernourished bodies rather than war-warped personalities, however, appeared to be the principal post-war problem faced by children interned at Bacolod. A follow-up study of boys and girls who spent their most impressionable years in an internment camp should be made to establish the real significance of this traumatic experience.

There were older children—teen agers and young adults —within the Bacolod camp. Among these romance blossomed, but feebly. Choice (real or imagined) in the selection of courtship partners is an essential aspect of the occidental courtship pattern, and such choice was lacking in the Bacolod setting.

An eighteen-year-old girl was interned shortly after the announcement by her parents of her engagement to a young army officer stationed in the Islands. Internment cut off communication between the girl and her fiancé. She began to keep constant company with one of the two young unmarried men in the camp, and there were rumors of their intended marriage. The lack of privacy in camp did not act as a deterrent to the romantic expressions of affection by the couple. Later, however, when the girl was moved to Santo Tomas where there was a wider selection of males, she transferred her attentions to someone else.

There was also in Bacolod a widower in his twenties with an infant son. A missionary, slightly older than the widower, "adopted" the baby. She prepared its food, washed its clothes, took constant care of both the infant and the father. Other internees expected the widower and the missionary to marry as soon as circumstances of peace permitted. Again, however, the known absence of choice in the selection of a mate seems to have been a factor. The widower married a girl he met immediately after release from internment.

The social setting for community government within the Bacolod camp and within war relocation centers in the United States was similar. In relocation centers "The problem of community government was the problem of [the] divergent geographic, economic, social, political, educational, and age groups . . . to achieve a true community of interest. . . . It was a problem of the need for creation of new values and social structure to meet the conditions of a new social and physical environment.

"The new environment into which the [Japanese] evacuees moved was one of uniformity in housing, food, employment and available services. Not so the people. . . . The social and cultural differences within the population were of more significance than were the similarities."[22]

Within the relocation centers there was conflict of the self-government by the Japanese evacuees with the administration of the War Relocation Authority. Efforts to extend to the evacuees greater measure of self-regulation and planning resulted in several administrative crises.

In attempting to explain the evacuee strikes and mass demonstrations which occurred in some of the relocation centers Leighton writes: "Out of the confusion of a community under stress there is likely to arise a single radical system of belief which may or may not bring a new stability, but which will bring to a large section of the population a sense of at least temporary relief from stress."[23] The experiment in the communal distribution of private property was the radical, non-aggressive system adopted by Bacolod internees as a means of temporary relief in crisis.

The urge for mere survival, normally subordinated in the complexities of civilized society, assumed primary importance in the Bacolod camp. In such a situation individual desires and fears identified themselves with group survival. There emerged a new group economic ideology in which group welfare superseded, for the time being, individu-

[22] *United States Department of the Interior*, War Relocation Authority, "Community Government in War Relocation Centers" (Washington, D.C., 1947), p. 14.
[23] Leighton, *op. cit.*, p. 302.

alistic rights of ownership. The group became the unit for survival or annihilation.

Severed from outside sources of aid, deprived of all assets except those at hand, individuals sought a modicum of personal security in group unification. Camp sentiment overwhelmingly favored the communal plan when it was adopted by popular vote. After several months of sharing, however, and evidence that the crisis situation was to be of longer duration than was at first anticipated, the fervor for group solidarity waned. Meditation replaced panic. The mere fact of survival helped to reestablish self-confidence, and in time individualism began to reassert itself.

The original communal program remained the majority opinion for the duration of the Bacolod camp and thus was the guiding principle of camp administration. However, the extent to which the group had a right to make demands upon the property and upon the time of the individual was questioned. The binding power of the decision to pool foodstuffs was questioned also. Would it be honest to take back personal supplies donated to the group under excitement and stress?

At this stage in the camp history pre-war concepts of "unselfishness," "human rights," "honesty and fair play" underwent scrutiny and redefinition. In some instances both the abstract interpretation and the practice of a concept changed. One of the most honest men in camp felt justified in stealing from the camp several cans of food pooled from his personal supplies.

In spite of individual digressions from the communal ownership plan, this voluntary social order was not abolished. The general recognition of internee interdependence went deeper than the sharing of canned goods. The "hads" (with regard to material goods) required the talents and services of the "had nots," for it was the "had nots" who converted the school building into livable camp quarters. Personal illness and misfortune struck "hads" and "had nots" indiscriminately. The afflicted were at the mercy of their associates.

The major camp problems related to the trinity of food, housing, health. Housing and health were not personal matters amenable to individual solution. Group responsibility for food became, in reality, a corollary to an unformulated system of mutual aid put into practice in the opening hours of camp with regard to housing and health.

Another factor which militated against private ownership of property in the Bacolod camp was the difficulty of protecting highly desirable goods from theft. There was an absence of police inspection and of facilities for concealing goods with safety. Pooled goods were stored in a small shed found on the grounds and repaired by internees for that purpose.

Whether the donor who pooled his food was dictated by altruistic regard for his associates or by anxiety for his own personal welfare at the hands of the group, the external evidences of group cohesion resulting from the pooling decision were the same. That diverse motivations often give the same end result is one of the great obstacles to theoretical conclusions regarding human actions.

The breakdown of economic and social barriers effected by internment encouraged the concrete expression of broad attitudes. Some individuals became articulate for the first time on such subjects as democracy, communism, racial and religious discrimination. In the camp assemblies opinions were freely expressed with regard to special privileges for the old, the sick, and children. An equally fruitful subject for discussion was the harmful effects which might arise from racial, religious, or economic discrimination within the interned group.

Largely by virtue of the new opportunity for self-expression afforded by internment a new leadership emerged from the assorted crowd. Strong characters came to the forefront. These followed no national, racial, or pre-war social and economic lines. The new leadership was based upon the presentation of ideologies and action patterns acceptable to the group and upon a willingness and capacity for immediate practical action.[24] Previous claims to eminence had to be reestablished.

Racial and national segregation were prohibited by the camp mode of living. The new intimacy between races seemed to result in the strengthening of present racial attitudes (when such attitudes were liberal) and in the modification and reversal of prejudicial attitudes. The selection of a racially and nationally mixed leadership indicated such a trend. There was abundant evidence that race, in itself, lost significance as the camp continued in operation. As a component part of a whole, each individual came to be accepted or rejected by the group according to his contributions to the group unit.

The Scotsman chosen by a group predominantly American was a quiet, middle aged, graying man whose American

---

[24] The authors of *The Peckham Experiment* note that when there is a lack of an organized program and of regulations of members of a group "they [the leaders] emerge naturally." Innes H. Pearse and Lucy H. Crocker, *The Peckham Experiment* (London: Allen and Unwin, Ltd., 1943), p. 128.

wife had gone to the States to place two daughters in school when war struck the Islands. It was his indication of greater concern for the group welfare than for his own which caused his election. Though opposition to the director's food policy arose later, he was at all times personally popular with white and dark skinned internees alike. He refused to accept for himself perquisites of any kind—extra space for his cot or extra servings in the dining room.

By a process of trial and error the kitchen supervision was shifted until the best qualified person emerged. For the original leadership of a woman experienced in feeding Americans was substituted that of one acquainted with native foods. In the camp gardening program familiarity with Philippine soils and plant growth was essential, and men nearest the Island culture—by birth, marriage, or pre-war occupation—were those who had this knowledge. In the field of domestic affairs a dark skinned Indian from an American reservation trained other women in laundering without soap and in re-using worn out garments as sewing materials.

Fifty-four per cent of the Bacolod adult male internees held administrative positions of one kind or another prior to the war. Obviously there were insufficient opportunities for all of these to direct camp work, had they been qualified to do so.

Pre-war executive experience in the handling of corporate affairs was in itself of no value to the camp, and often such experience became a handicap to the personal adjustment of the individuals concerned. This was true when the conscious loss of pre-war status was not accompanied by a compensating sense of prestige within the interned group. The absence of monetary reward discouraged a few would-be leaders. The interracial, cross-sectional leadership which did arise was directed toward the goal of group service and not personal gain.

It appears that the following conclusions can be drawn. Disruptive effects followed the adoption of new culture traits, but women seemed to adapt themselves to the internment situation more readily than did male internees. Filipino men, women, and children and others who had lived with Filipinos and had adopted Island habits also found internment less difficult than did those who had held themselves aloof from the Island culture. Orientals found adjustment easier with regard to (a) the camp food, (b) the absence of privacy, and (c) cultural anxieties about the future. Among occidentals the missionaries (as contrasted with lay groups) and young men (as contrasted with those over fifty) experienced fewer post-war anxieties during internment.

Young children did not experience in the internment situation the subjective feeling of frustration which was characteristic of adults. Being housed with their mothers the children's sense of security was unshaken. In periods of extreme peril, e.g., the shelling of Santo Tomas camp by the Japanese, it was officially recognized that there was less hysteria and disorder in the children's quarters than in those occupied by adults alone.

The drive for security resulted in an internment ideology that approved the equalization of property. Leadership in the communal, cooperative camp society cut across national, racial, and cultural lines. The internment situation afforded opportunity for the expression of capabilities held dormant in a technological, highly stratified social order.

Dr. E. H. Spicer, Head of the Community Analysis Division of the War Relocation Authority has commented: "There seems to be a basic similarity in what happens to all groups placed in artificial communities of the relocation center or the internment camp type."[25] There is need for additional studies of such situations, with emphasis on the effects of the thwarting of basic and acquired drives upon personality and upon group organization. From other such analyses, checked by different observers, there should come an ultimate theory of internment with the possibility of scientific social forecasting of individual and group responses in situations where mobility, association, and general conduct are rigidly controlled.

[25] E. H. Spicer. Letter addressed to Dr. Gordon W. Blackwell, Director of the Institute for Research in Social Science, University of North Carolina, Chapel Hill, N.C., March 26, 1946.

————◄◄ Bibliography ►►——

Allport, G. W., et al. "Personality Under Social Catastrophe: An Analysis of 90 German Life Histories," *Character and Personality*, x, 1-22.

Allport, G. W., and Postman, Leo. *The Psychology of Rumor* (New York: Henry Holt & Co., 1947).

Ambrière, Francis. *The Long Holiday* (Chicago: Ziff-Davis Co., 1947).

"American and Allied Personnel Recovered from Japanese Prisons," *Army Forces Western Pacific* (Manila: November 11, 1945).

"American-Philippine Trade Relations," *Report of the Technical Committee to the President of the Philippines* (Washington, D.C., 1944).

Annals of the American Academy of Political and Social Science, "The Netherlands During German Occupation," ccxlv (May, 1946).

Army and Navy Journal. lxxxiii (February 17, 1945).

Bettelheim, Bruno. "Individual and Mass Behavior in Extreme Situations," *Journal of Abnormal and Social Psychology*, xxxviii (1943), 417-452.

Bondy, Curt. "Buchenwald, Germany," *Journal of Abnormal and Social Psychology*, xxxviii (1943), 453-457.

Bulletin of the American Internees' Committee (San Francisco, March 28, 1946).

Burney, Christopher. *The Dungeon Democracy* (New York: Duell, Sloan & Pearce, 1946).

"Camp Maloney," *Rotarian*, lxvi (March, 1945), 20-21.

Cannon, Walter B. *Bodily Changes in Pain, Hunger, Fear and Rage* (New York: D. Appleton, 1916).

Caplow, Theodore. "Rumors in War," *Social Forces*, xxv (March, 1947), 298-302.

Close, Kathryn. "They Want to Be People," *Survey Graphic*, xxxv (November, 1946), 392-395.

Cohen, Israel. *The Ruhleben Prison Camp* (London: Methuen & Co., Ltd., 1917).

"Commonwealth of the Philippines," *Statesman's Year Book*, LXXXI (1944), 672-678.

Cooley, C. H. *Human Nature and the Social Order* (New York: Scribner's, 1902).

Cummings, E. E. *The Enormous Room* (New York: Boni & Liveright, 1922).

de Terente, Violette C. "I Was Interned Forty-Six Months," *Christian Science Monitor Magazine Section* (December 9, 1944).

Douglas, J. Harvey. *Captured* (New York: Doran & Co., 1918).

Edman, Irwin. *Human Traits and Their Social Significance* (Boston: Houghton Mifflin Co., 1920).

Elliott, Mabel and Merrill, Francis. *Social Disorganization* (New York: Harper & Brothers, 1941).

Embree, John F. "Causes of Unrest at Relocation Centers," Community Analysis Report No. 2, *United States Department of the Interior*, War Relocation Authority, 1943.

Ford, Carey, and MacBain, Alastair. *The Last Time I Saw Them* (New York: Scribner's, 1946).

Freud, Anna, and Burlingham, Dorothy T. *War and Children* (New York: Medical War Books, 1943).

Gellhorn, Martha. "The Undefeated," *Collier's Magazine*, CXV (March 3, 1945), 42.

Gillin, John. "Acculturation and Personality," *American Sociological Review*, V (1940), 371-380.

Gillin, John. "Custom and Range of Human Response," *Character and Personality*, XIII (December, 1944), 101-134.

"Green and Legal Curragh," *New Yorker*, XIX (June 19, 1943), 52.

Green, Arthur. *Story of a Prisoner of War* (London: Chatto & Windus, 1916).

Harrison, Earl H. "Civilian Internment—American Way," *Survey Graphic*, XXXIII (May, 1944), 229-233.

"Health of Children in Occupied Europe," *International Labor Office* (Montreal, 1943).

Hélion, Jean. *They Shall Not Have Me* (New York: E. P. Dutton Co., 1943).

"History of Santo Tomas," American National Red Cross, *Prisoner of War Bulletin*, II (April, 1944), 4.

Jacobi, Jolan. *The Psychology of Jung* (New Haven: Yale University Press, 1943).

Joint Army-Navy Intelligence Service Report No. 154 (Washington, D.C., 1944).

Kardiner, Abram. *Psychological Frontiers of Society* (New York: Columbia University Press, 1945).

Keith, Agnes Newton. "All Are Guilty," *Atlantic Monthly*, CLXXVIII (August, 1946), 43-46.

Keith, Agnes Newton. "Three Came Home," *Atlantic Monthly*, CLXXVII (February, 1946), 39-47.

Keith, Agnes Newton. *Three Came Home* (Boston: Little, Brown Co., 1947).

Koestler, Arthur. *Scum of the Earth* (New York: Macmillan, 1941).

Korner, Ija. "The Psychological Needs of the Individual Dissolving in the Mass and the Possibilities of Clinical Help," *Journal of Social Psychology*, XVI (1942), 143-150.

Leighton, A. H. *The Governing of Men* (Princeton: Princeton University Press, 1946).

Liggett, Eugene. "Religion," *Time*, XLVI (December 31, 1945), 52.

Linton, Ralph. *The Cultural Background of Personality* (New York: Appleton-Century Co., 1945).

Linton, Ralph. *The Study of Man* (New York: Appleton-Century Co., 1936).

Lipscomb, F. M. "Medicine," *Time*, XLVI (November 5, 1945), 60.

Lundberg, George A. "Can Science Save Us?" *Harper's*, CXCI (December, 1945), 525-531.

Macaraig, Serafin E. "Social Attitudes of Filipinos toward Foreigners in the Philippines," *Philippine Social Science Review*, XI (1939), 26-33.

McCall, J. E. *Santo Tomas Internment Camp* (Lincoln: Woodruff Printing Co., 1945).

McCoy, M. H., et al. *Ten Escape from Tojo* (New York: Farrar & Rinehart, 1944).

Mahoney, Henry C. *Sixteen Months in Four German Prisons* (London: Sampson, Low, Marston Co., 1917).

Maslow, A. H. "Conflict, Frustration and the Theory of Threat," *Journal of Abnormal and Social Psychology,* XXXVIII (1943), 81-86.

Maurer, Rose. *Soviet Health Care in Peace and War* (New York: American Russian Institute, 1943).

Mead, Margaret. *Sex and Temperament in Three Primitive Societies* (New York: William Morrow Co., 1935).

Mydans, Shelley. *The Open City* (Garden City: Doubleday Co., 1945).

Nerac, Eleanore. "Refugee in Internment," *Independent Woman,* XXI (April, 1942), 113-114.

Newman, P. H. "The Prisoner-of-War Mentality," *British Medical Journal,* I (January 1, 1944), 8ff.

O'Kubo, Miné. *Citizen 13660* (New York: Columbia University Press, 1946).

Overholser, Winfred. "Rescue from Starvation," *Survey Graphic,* XXXI (December, 1942), 596-598.

Pearse, Innes H., and Crocker, Lucy H. *The Peckham Experiment* (London: Allen and Unwin, Ltd., 1943).

Porteus, S. D. *Temperament and Race* (Boston: Richard Badger Co., 1926).

Pritchard, Rosemary, and Rosenzweig, Saul. "The Effects of War Stress Upon Childhood and Youth," *Journal of Abnormal and Social Psychology,* XXXVIII (1942), 329-344.

"Quiet Life in Hampshire," *New Yorker,* XXII (March 2, 1946), 48-57.

"Report of Claims Committee," *Liberated Military Personnel* (American Bldg., Washington, D.C., 1946).

Rojo, Trinidad A. "Philippine Population Problems," *Philippine Social Science Review,* XI (1929), 134-152.

Rousset, David. *The Other Kingdom* (New York: Reynal & Hitchcock, 1947).

Shaffer, Laurance F. *The Psychology of Adjustment* (Boston: Houghton Mifflin Co., 1936).

Sheridan, R. E. *Recollections of Four Years, 1941-1945* (Manila: La Salle College, 1946).

Smith, William A. "In Weihsien Prison Camp," *Asia and the Americas*, XLVI (July, 1946), 318-323.

Sneed, Bessie. *Captured by the Japanese* (Denver: Bradford-Robinson Co., 1946).

Sorokin, P. A. *Man and Society in Calamity* (New York: Dutton & Co., 1942).

Soupalt, Philippe. *Age of Assassins* (New York: Alfred A. Knopf, 1946).

Spanton, E. F. *In German Gaols* (London: Society for Promoting Christian Knowledge, 1917).

Stevens, F. H. *Santo Tomas* (New York: Stratford House, 1946).

Stevens, N. W. "Out of the Depths," *Independent Woman*, XXIV (February, 1945), 44.

Szmaglewska, Seweryna. *Smoke over Birkenau* (New York: Henry Holt & Co., 1947).

Terry, Carol. *Kept* (Philadelphia: Ramabai Mukti Mission, 1945).

Thomas, Dorothy S., and Nishimoto, R. S. *The Spoilage* (Berkeley, Calif.: Univ. of California Press, 1946).

"Treaties, Conventions, International Acts, Protocols," *United States Senate Document No. 134*, IV (1938), 5229-5250.

United States Department of Commerce, Bureau of the Census. "Foreign Born and Mixed Population of the Philippines, by Provinces, 1939." Washington, D.C.

United States Department of the Interior, War Relocation Authority, Washington, D.C., 1947:

    (1) Administrative Highlights of the WRA Program

    (2) Community Government in War Relocation Centers

    (3) Evacuated People, The—A Quantitative Description

    (4) Impounded People—Japanese Americans in the Relocation Centers

    (5) Legal and Constitutional Phases of the War Relocation Authority Program

    (6) Relocation Program, The

    (7) Wartime Exile—The Exclusion of the Japanese Americans from the West Coast

    (8) WRA, A Story of Human Conservation

Vaughan, Elizabeth H. "Adjustment Problems in a Concentration Camp," *Sociology and Social Research*, XXXII, (September, 1947), 513-518.

Walker, E. R. C. "Impressions of a Repatriated Medical Officer," *Lancet*, 1 (April 15, 1944), 514.

Ward, R. S. *Asia for the Asiatics?* (Chicago: University of Chicago Press, 1945).

"What Can Be Done with String," American National Red Cross, *Prisoner of War Bulletin*, 1 (July, 1943), 6.

Wittkower, E., and Spillane, J. P. "Neuroses in War," *British Medical Journal*, 1 (1940), 223.

Woodworth, R. S. *Adjustment and Mastery* (Baltimore: Williams and Wilkins, 1933).

Young, Kimball. "Population and Power: Some Comments on Demographic Changes in Europe," *Social Forces*, XXV (October, 1946), 1-9.

Zweig, Stefan. *Mary Queen of Scotland and the Isles* (New York: Viking Press, 1935).

————◄◄ Appendix ►►————

LIST OF BOOKS IN THE LIBRARY OF CONGRESS
ON GERMAN PRISON CAMPS*

October 2, 1918   Chief Bibliographer

1. Andre Georges. *Ma Captivité en Allemagne 1914-1917.* Paris, 1918.
2. Austin, Lorimer J. *My Experiences as a German Prisoner,* London. A. Melrose, Ltd., 1915.
3. Blanchin, L. *Chez Eux: Souvenirs de Guerre et de Captivité.* Paris, Delgrave, 1916.
4. Close, Percy L. *A Prisoner of Germans in South-west Africa.* London. T. F. Unwin, Ltd., 1916.
5. Cohen, Israel. *The Ruhleben Prison Camp: A Record of Nineteen Months' Internment.* London: Methuen and Company, Ltd., 1917.
6. Davies, Alfred T. *Student Captives.* An account of the work of the British prisoners of war book scheme (educational). Leicester. Stevens and Son. 1917.
7. Doitsh, E. *The First Springbok Prisoner in Germany.* London. McBride, Nast and Company, Ltd., 1917.
8. Douglas, J. H. *Captured.* New York, George H. Doran Company. 1918.
9. Doyle, Sir Arthur C. *The Story of British Prisoners.* London. The Central Committee for National Patriotic Organization, 1915.
10. Great Britain Foreign Office. *Correspondence with the German Government Respecting the Death by Burning of J. P. Genower, Able Seaman, When Prisoner of War at Bradenburg Camp.* London. H. M. Stationery Office, 1918.
11. ——*Correspondence with the United States Ambassador Respecting the Treatment of British Prisoners of War and Interned Civilians in Germany.* London. H. M. Stationery Office, 1915.

* Appendix is copied directly from list supplied by the Library of Congress.

12.   ——*Further Correspondence with the United States Ambassador*. London. H. M. Stationery Office, 1915.

13.   ——*Correspondence with the United States Ambassador Respecting Conditions in the Internment Camp at Ruhleben*. London. H. M. Stationery Office, 1916.

14.   ——*Correspondence with the United States Ambassador Respecting the Treatment of British Prisoners of War and Interned Civilians in Germany*. London. H. M. Stationery Office, 1915.

15.   ——*Further Correspondence Respecting Conditions of Diet and Nutrition in the Internment Camp at Ruhleben and the Proposed Release of Interned Civilians*. London. H. M. Stationery Office. 1916.

16.   ——*Further Correspondence with the United States Ambassador Respecting the Treatment of British Prisoners of War and Interned Civilians in Germany*. London. H. M. Stationery Office, 1916.

17.   ——*Further Correspondence with the United States Ambassador Respecting the Treatment of British Prisoners of War and Interned Civilians in Germany*. London. H. M. Stationery Office, 1916.

18.   ——*Reports on the Treatment by the Germans of British Prisoners and Natives in German East Africa*. London. H. M. Stationery Office, 1917.

19.   ——*Government Committee on Treatment by the Enemy of British Prisoners of War*. The Horrors of Wittenberg; Official Report to the British Government. London. C. A. Pearson, Ltd., 1916.

20.   ——*Report on the Treatment by the Enemy of British Prisoners of War Regarding the Conditions Obtaining at Wittenberg Camp during the Typhus Epidemic of 1915*. H. M. Stationery Office. London, 1916.

21.   ——*Report on the Typhus Epidemic at Gardelegen during the Spring and Summer of 1915*. London. H. M. Stationery Office. 1916.

22.   Green, Arthur. *The Story of a Prisoner of War*. London. Chatto and Windus, 1916.

23. Hennebois, Charles. *In German Hands*. London. W. Heinemann, 1916.

24. ——*Journal d'un Grand Blessé*. Paris. Plon-Nourrit et Cie, 1916.

25. ——*In the Hands of the Huns*. London. S. Marshall, H. Kint and Company, Ltd., 1916.

26. Jeffery, J. E. *Servants of the Guns*. London. Smith, Elder and Company, 1917.

27. McCarthy, D. J. *The Prisoner of War in Germany*. New York. Moffat, Yard and Company, 1917.

28. Mahoney, H. C. *Interned in Germany*. New York. R. M. McBride and Company, 1918.

29. ——*Sixteen Months in Four German Prisons*. London and Edinburgh. S. Low, Marston and Company, Ltd., 1917.

30. Marshall, L. *Experiences in German Gaols*. Liverpool. The Liverpool Booksellers Company, Ltd., 1915.

31. Martin, Jean. *Captivity and Escape*. Translated by Miss V. A. Randell. London. J. Murray, 1917.

32. O'Brien, Pat. *Outwitting the Hun: My Escape from a German Prison Camp*. New York: Harper and Brothers, 1918.

33. O'Rorke, B. G. *In the Hands of the Enemy*. London, and New York. Longmans, Green and Company, 1915.

34. Pearson, George. *The Escape of the Princess Pat*. New York. George H. Doran Company, 1918.

35. Pyke, Geoffrey. *To Ruhleben—and Back*. London. Constable and Company, Ltd., 1916.

36. Riou, Gaston. *The Diary of a French Private*. Translated from the French by Edna and Dedar Paul. London, G. Allen and Unwin, Ltd., 1916.

37. ——*Journal d'un Simple Soldat*. Paris. Hachette et Cie, 1916.

38. Sladen, D. B. W. (editor). *In Ruhleben, Letters from a Prisoner to His Mother*. London. Hurst and Blackett, Ltd., 1917.

39. Spanton, E. P. *In German Gaols*. London. Society for Promoting Christian Knowledge, 1917.

40. ———*The Treatment of Prisoners of War in England and Germany during the First Eight Months of the War.* London. H. M. Stationery Office, 1915.

41. United States Legation. Great Britain. *Reports by the United States Officials on the Treatment of British Prisoners of War and Interned Civilians at Certain Places of Detention in Germany.* London. H. M. Stationery Office, 1915.

42. Warnod, Andre. *Prisoner of War.* Translated by M. Jourdain. London. W. Heinemann, 1916.

43. ———*Wounded and a Prisoner of War.* New York. George H. Doran Company, 1917.

44. Zavie, Emile. *Prisonniers en Allemagne.* Paris. Chapelot, 1917.

◀◀ Index ▶▶